To Gradma

I Love

a pocketful of

RHYME

Imagination for a new generation

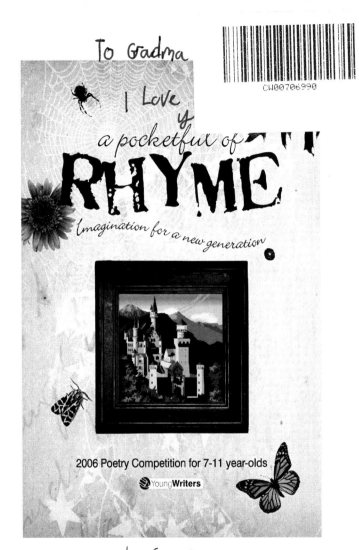

2006 Poetry Competition for 7-11 year-olds

YoungWriters

Love from
chloe

Inspirations From Kent
Edited by Mark Richardson

the Best Grandma
in the
would

 Young**Writers**

First published in Great Britain in 2007 by:
Young Writers
Remus House
Coltsfoot Drive
Peterborough
PE2 9JX
Telephone: 01733 890066
Website: www.youngwriters.co.uk

SB ISBN 1 84602 729 2

Foreword

Young Writers was established in 1991 and has been passionately devoted to the promotion of reading and writing in children and young adults ever since. The quest continues today. Young Writers remains as committed to the nurturing of poetic and literary talent as ever.

This year's Young Writers competition has proven as vibrant and dynamic as ever and we are delighted to present a showcase of the best poetry from across the UK and in some cases overseas. Each poem has been selected from a wealth of *A Pocketful Of Rhyme* entries before ultimately being published in this, our fourteenth primary school poetry series.

Once again, we have been supremely impressed by the overall quality of the entries we have received. The imagination, energy and creativity which has gone into each young writer's entry made choosing the poems a challenging and often difficult but ultimately hugely rewarding task - the general high standard of the work submitted ensured this opportunity to bring their poetry to a larger appreciative audience.

We sincerely hope you are pleased with this final collection and that you will enjoy *A Pocketful Of Rhyme Inspirations From Kent* for many years to come.

Contents

Kingsdown & Ringwould CEP School

Megan Fisher (10)	15
Emily Brookes (10)	16
Rebecca Stagg (10)	16
Sarah Carlotti (10)	17
Charys Dewhurst (10)	17
Isabel Castle (10)	18
Tabitha Shepherd (10)	19
Amy Brown (10)	20
Tara Hodgkins (10)	20
Alannah Taylor (10)	21
Amy Miller (10)	21
Jessica Henry (10)	22
Micheal Wright (10)	22
Ellenor Hadlow (10)	23
Roman Gronkowski (11)	23
William Sparrow (10)	24
Jennifer Trower (10)	24
Mollie Letheren-Smith (10)	24
Jack Mashford (10)	25
Andrew White (10)	25
Chloe Brown (10)	26

Offham CP School

Paige Garrett (8)	26
Stanley Draper (8)	26
Joshua Burford (8)	27
Clarissa Price (10)	27
Katrine Khomitch (8)	27
James Turner (8)	28
Elizabeth Berman (8)	28
Josh Haselden (8)	28
Hanah Ahmed (8)	29
Lucy Christmas (8)	29
Kathryn Parker (8)	29
Melissa Seabrook (8)	30
Erin Baker (8)	30
Jacob Hancock (8)	30
Benjamin Chapman (11)	31
Elynor Alderton (8)	31
Dan Chapman (8)	31

Caitlin Foxell (8)	32
Jack Davis (11)	32
Jack Brown (8)	32
Vivien Hadlow (10)	33
Oliver Haselden (11)	33
Yasmin-Hanna Ryan (10)	34
Jack Ball (10)	34
Maxim Gorham (10)	34

Our Lady of Hartley RC Primary School

Danny Green-Ryan (10)	35
Liam Spurin (10)	35
Zac Maidment (10)	36
Lara Paton (9)	36
Megan Skey (9)	37
Lewis Wright (10)	37
Padraig Flaherty (10)	38
Katie McCaughey (10)	38
Jeffrey Horscroft (11)	39
Sarah Day (9)	39
Eleanor Sparling (11)	40
Thomas Gibbins	40
Juan Miguel Cabling (10)	41
Ella Cooper (8)	41
Alice Steingass (10)	42
Hannah Gillespie (9)	42
Billy Goldsmith (10)	43
Michael Gardiner (9)	43
Dheelan Sydamah (10)	44
Catherine Rye (8)	44
Zofia Gawor (10)	45
Charlie Scott Flint (10)	46
Ella Marriner (10)	46
Henry Goodwin (10)	47
Maria Gemmell (10)	48
Ella Shire (10)	49
James Gilhooly (9)	50
Aaron Carlse (10)	50
Joshua Price (10)	51
Joe Scott (10)	51

Rolvenden Primary School

Oscar Betts (9)	74
Robert Ward (9)	75
Millie Goad (9)	75
Rebecca Talbot (9)	76
Rosie Masters (9)	76
Kelly Ann Hedges (9)	77
Luke Piggott (10)	77
Rhianna Hodgkins (9)	78
Jacky Hunt (10)	78
Kajun Stannard (8)	78

Shernold School

Joanna Harvey (10)	79
Katie Swift (9)	80
Laura Morton (8)	80
Thomas Collins (8)	81
George Quinn (8)	81
Daniel Sharp (10)	82
Connor Rumball (9)	82
Aaliyah Buxy (7)	83
Anujan Ravishankar (7)	83
Lilyan Mashallah (8)	84
Constance Fury (7)	84
Jemima Burn (7)	84
Amelia Lucy Gregory (7)	85
Bethany Joanne Tompsett (7)	85
Keri Mo (7)	86
Rebecca-Kate Lawley Watts (9)	86
Robert Lawrence (10)	87
Vinnie Iandolo (7)	87
Jasmine Ede (9)	88
Zenon Ede (7)	88
Garren Beaulieu (10)	89
Danielle Wheat (10)	89
Abbie Prentice (10)	90
George Durrant (9)	90
Chloe Rogers (8)	91
Anna Holness (7)	91
Sophie Burn (10)	92
Ellena Jepheart (8)	92

Chloe Funnell (10)	93
Jack Bates (10)	93
Jasmin Major (8)	94
Isabelle Knight (7)	94
Dominic Le Lion (10)	95
Charlotte Wilson (8)	95
Matilda Duffy (10)	96
Jack Wilson (8)	96
Gemma Levy (10)	97
Jade Richards (7)	97
Isabel Peterson (7)	98
Alice Jepheart (10)	98
Natalie Ashby (8)	99
Alex Elliott (9)	100
Ahsen Ustaóglu (10)	100
Ruth Arnett (9)	101
Ali Sever (9)	102
Jacob Bischoff (7)	102
Charlotte Rugg-Gunn (8)	103
James Sharp (9)	103
Maisy Cane (8)	104
Ellis Iandolo (9)	104
Amelia C Peterson (9)	105
Elizabeth Elliott (7)	105
Chelsea Lauren Davison (9)	106
Harry Grindle (8)	106
Emily Watts (9)	107
Miriam Aziz (9)	107
Sam Farmer (9)	108
Charlotte Beedell (9)	109
Jordan Tompsett (10)	110
Megan Smith (8)	110
Elisabeth Holness (10)	111

The Holy Family Catholic Primary School

Shanice Friday (11)	111
Beth White (10)	112
Lauren Ramsden (10)	112

The Poems

My Brother

My brother is a sizzling sausage that has been burnt by the sun
He is the diamond in the dirt that hasn't been found
He is a fresh rose picked from a greenhouse in South East London
He is the smell of fresh bananas picked from the Caribbean
He's the taste of fresh steak from Ireland
He is a crazy monkey climbing in the rainforest
As I said before, he is the diamond in the dirt that hasn't been found.

Louis Bellett (9)
Bursted Wood Primary School

My Gorgeous Mum

My mum is gorgeous like sun-ripe delicious plums.
Her lips are as red as cherry tomatoes as she smears red lipstick
Her eyes are as glittery as the sunlight beaming down towards her
Her hands twinkle like stars through the daylight
She is as soft as pillowcases lying on top of each other
She is never vague, she is always as calm as can be
My mother is my hero, she is as motherly as can be.

Sasha Seehra (9)
Bursted Wood Primary School

My Dad

He is creamy mashed potato,
He is a cute but dangerous hedgehog,
He is a windy autumn day,
He is a chestnut in an armour-green coat,
An old beautiful tree,
He is a bunch of yellow bananas,
He smells of fresh mint.

Lauren Webber (9)
Bursted Wood Primary School

My Sister Kirsty

She is a bright red, hot chilli,
My sister is a wild cat that is fast but sly,
She is a strong character,
A bright yellow banana,
My sister is a honeycomb,
She is flexible jelly,
My sister is pink blossom in the breeze,
She is a caring, loving sister.

Danny Holloway (9)
Bursted Wood Primary School

My Sister Shelby

She is a sweet lollipop,
She is a strong ship,
She is a massive pickle,
She is a bendy, flexible banana,
A special blossom in the breeze,
She is a fast jaguar,
She is the summer sun,
She is a tulip,
She is a daisy,
She is a beautiful sunflower.

Lillie Waters (10)
Bursted Wood Primary School

My Cousin

My cousin is a gumdrop, sweet not sour,
She's bananas, I really mean it!
She's a jaguar, strong and swift,
A beautiful blossom swaying in the breeze,
She is a soft blanket that I can hold when I'm alone,
She's the sun to dry out my tears,
She's my cousin and always will be.

Thomas Brown (10)
Bursted Wood Primary School

My Dad

My dad is loud but not tall,
In fact he is quite small,
He is a bear because he's strong,
But when it's an answer he's wrong.

My dad is a wolf, full-blood wild,
But he can be just like a child,
He isn't tall,
But isn't that small,
In fact he's in the middle of them all.

Blair Anderson (9)
Bursted Wood Primary School

My Sister

My sister is a big red rose
Also she's a ferocious dog
My sister is a bouncy chair
But sometimes she is a tiger
My sister is a giggle box
And also a chatterbox.

Jason Robins (10)
Bursted Wood Primary School

My Mum

She's a bright banana,
She is a soft loaf of bread,
She's a tall runner bean,
She's a soft bear,
A nice person and a super woman,
The smell of juicy pineapple,
She's a sweetie pie.

Manpreet Ghuman (9)
Bursted Wood Primary School

My Brother

He is a bright yellow banana,
His hair is a pineapple,
A bright white cauliflower,
A special PS2 player on the computer,
A hairy monkey
He's a strong little flea,
He's jolly in the summer but grumpy in the winter
And he really hates flowers.

Jimmy Brooker (9)
Bursted Wood Primary School

My Sister Samantha

She's a cheeky monkey
Very sweet sometimes.
Smarter than me, smarter than a horse.
She is a thin sugarcane,
She's a fast runner bean,
A silly sausage.
A good dramatic, drama queen,
She's a fun girl,
She is cooler than a dog,
A funky dancer.

Hannah Marie Goulding (9)
Bursted Wood Primary School

My Nan

She is a kind bird, as sweet as can be
She is a beautiful smelling rose
She is a singing hummingbird
She is funny and makes me laugh
She is the sun rising ever so gracefully
She is the sun.

Megan Parsons (9)
Bursted Wood Primary School

My Cousin Hayley

My cousin Hayley is an angel who came down to Earth
Hayley is a delicate and fragile china plate
She is a soft, pure white feather
Hayley can be cheeky, a lively monkey then a silent star, shining in
the moonlit sky

My cousin is a playful lion cub on the hot savannah
My Hayley is a big, soft, cuddly teddy bear she is a soft, hot, creamy
chocolate bar

Her eyes are blue as ocean waves
Hayley is a sweet-smelling red rose
She is a warm blanket that I can snuggle up with
She is a bright sun who dries up my tears
Her smile is a crescent moon, smiling in the sky
She is a sudden downpour bursting from the grey skies
when she cries.

Holly Ellen Tavender (9)
Bursted Wood Primary School

My Brother

My brother is,
Nowhere near as caring as my mother,
But I'm still happy,
He's my brother.

His curly hair,
Is like a mop.
It's very weird,
Cos it's straight on top.
He's always very funny,
But not as funny as my mother,
But just as much as I love my mum,
I also love my brother.

Ben Povey (9)
Bursted Wood Primary School

My Super Cousin Alex

My cousin Alex is an extremely fast cheetah
My cousin Alex is a super strong gorilla
My cousin Alex has a hawk's eyesight
My cousin Alex is a terrifically tall giraffe
My cousin Alex is as angry as a great white
My cousin Alex is the perfect cousin for me.

My cousin Alex is greater than the Greek gods
My cousin Alex is the best athlete in the family
My cousin Alex is the strongest to me.
My cousin Alex is the giant in the family
My cousin Alex is the best cousin in the whole world.

Noah Gosbee (10)
Bursted Wood Primary School

My Brother

My brother is a speedy falcon
My brother is a bouncy chair
My brother is a playful puppy
My brother is a juicy burger
My brother is an angel
My brother is an excited cheetah
My brother is a speeding rocket
My brother is as long as a piece of wood.

Bradley Hales (10)
Bursted Wood Primary School

My Dad

His feet are smellier than cheese,
He's bigger than a 4x4 car,
The smell of a juicy pineapple,
The colour of a yellow jumper,
He's a bright leaf,
He's a lovely chocolate bar.

Jacob Marks (9)
Bursted Wood Primary School

My Uncle/Brother

My uncle is a piece of log
He always drives in the fog
He is a big man and he is fat
And he really wants a cat.

My brother is a fat sumo
He is a bear growling
He is a naughty bully, hitting
And he is an ugly witch.

Kerthan Srividiyakaran (10)
Bursted Wood Primary School

My Cousin

My cousin is a jacket potato,
A poisonous snake,
A fried chicken,
A piece of pie,
A monkey in a Christmas tree,
Some shouts and screams without a doubt,
He's an autumn mouse,
He sleeps in a junkyard of toys,
That's my cousin for sure.

Jonathan Cuthbert (9)
Bursted Wood Primary School

My Dad

A green runner bean,
A hot chilli,
A white grain of rice.

He's a soft winter evening
He's a big cheeky monkey.

Lydia Gorringe (10)
Bursted Wood Primary School

My Annoying Brother

My brother is so annoying,
He is very boring,
He is a devil,
His name is Neville,
And is a horse that's boring.

My brother is such a wimp,
He is a shy old chimp,
'Pack it in,'
I screamed at him,
When he made me a shy old chimp!

My brother suddenly cried,
'Oh God, please give me pride,
Everyone hates me,
Cos I'm a nasty flea,
That never wants to hide.'

I rushed to my brother,
And said, 'Hey don't bother,
You're not as bad,
As our grumpy old dad,
That is a stubborn old gorilla!'

Jasmine Chin (9)
Bursted Wood Primary School

My Mum

She is a soft loaf of bread,
She's a sweetie pie,
Her hair is a feather,
She's a red tomato,
Her nails are long green beans,
Her eyes are big bananas,
She's a beautiful red rose.

Tilly McCombie (9)
Bursted Wood Primary School

My Dad Is A Rock Star

My dad is a rock star
He is a big, tasty chocolate bar.
He's always slamming on his guitar
Oh, he's a rock star.

He is quite a wise owl
He is a man who is never that foul
He cannot sing as he only goes *lah*
Oh, he is a rock star.

My dad is ever, ever so silly
As he loves eating really hot chillies
He is a giant cuddly bear
He is the best dad who could ever be there.

Jessica Kingdon (10)
Bursted Wood Primary School

My Parents

My mum is a rose waving in the wind.
My mum is a cannon ball when she is mad,
My mum is a branch when she swishes her hair,
My mum is pretty like Cleopatra, mighty queen of Egypt.
My mum is like a mermaid singing her melody,
My mum is a barrier that protects me everywhere.

My dad is a tiger when he is angry,
My dad is like a partner that is always there,
My dad is a good person, stopping all chaos,
My dad is a gem I wouldn't trade for the world.
My dad is a giant teddy bear because he's cuddly,
My dad is a great man that I'll love for evermore.

Jordan Turner (10)
Bursted Wood Primary School

My Mum

My mum is a monster, big and hairy
All of my friends think that she is quite scary
She wakes me up every night
Giving me the world's biggest fright
She has three big and hairy noses
Sometimes for dinner she eats red roses
I like to wrap my hands round her hips
And kiss her big fat chunky lips.

Bethanie Austin (9)
Bursted Wood Primary School

Super Princess

Super princess is so bright,
She is always flying in the night.
She is always soaring around,
Until her feet touch the ground.
She is always twirling in the air,
But nobody seems to care.

Lauren Parker (9)
Eastry CE Primary School

Moon

Dry, cold, shiny and grey
Not much gravity,
Comes out every day,
It's so hard and so bumpy,
It changes into different shapes,
It floats in the sky,
It's so bright
And I see it in the night.

Bethany Dale (9)
Eastry CE Primary School

Young Writers - A Pocketful Of Rhyme Inspirations From Kent

The Man On The Moon

I once met a man,
Who had a van,
Who lived on the moon,
I will see him very soon,
His house is made of crust,
It is full of dust.

It was the day,
We had to go that way,
To the moon,
I will see him very soon,
I put a flower in my pocket,
Come on, time to get into the rocket.

Zoom,
Off they went, *boom*,
We landed on the moon,
I gave him a flower,
His house looked like a tower.

Scarlett Watson (9)
Eastry CE Primary School

Something Green

I saw a monster that was very mean,
Its body was large and dark green.
Its nostrils produced hot white steam
I think it was the scariest thing I've ever seen.
It wailed and hollered and let out a scream,
Then I woke up from a horrible dream.

I saw a monster that was big and red
And his favourite hobby was to go to bed.
It loves to read and write,
It plays rugby at night.

James Hunt (9)
Eastry CE Primary School

Open The Door

(Based on 'The Door' by Miroslav Holub)

Open the door,
Maybe outside there is
A pig with wings,
A talking apple,
Or a blue sun.

Open the door,
Maybe a dog will kiss a cat,
Maybe you'll see
A walking fish,
A dinosaur,
Or a flying pineapple.

If there's a ghost,
It will fly away.

Open the door,
Even if there is only a deadly flower,
Even there is only a pink banana,
Even if nothing is there,
At least there will be a draught.

Taryn Nanjiani (10)
Eastry CE Primary School

Moon

The man in the moon,
Will be out very soon,
He loves to eat cheese,
So give me some please,
He lives in the sky,
And loves to fly.

Laura Deveson (9)
Eastry CE Primary School

My Trip To The Moon

I have lots of lumps,
And big round bumps
I am dark grey
And I am not afraid.

I am going to the moon,
On a big round balloon,
I will play a tune,
On my big bassoon,
Until we reach the moon.

When we get there,
We will have a great feast,
And I will share it with my niece,
And with all the people I meet.

I go down with a bang,
Whoosh, crack, vroom, vroom, voom,
Then I land back on the moon
Looking like a buffoon.

Liam Luckhurst (9)
Eastry CE Primary School

The Wyvern

He has a tail as long as ten buses
His teeth are as sharp as carving knives
His eyes are a bright shade of green
They'll see you a mile away.

He likes to lie in the sun
He has lots of gems in a cave in the mountain
He likes to swim in the Nile
He has wings the size of buildings.

James Waldron (9)
Eastry CE Primary School

My Trip To The Moon

I'm going to the moon,
Suddenly, my rocket went zoom!
I have always wanted to go to the moon,
And now it is like a dream come true!

Crackle and crunch, I have landed on the moon,
Then when I got out I heard a loud boom,
For it was my heavy boots!
I locked my rocket, it toots!

When I walked about 50 yards,
I saw a green thing,
With five arms and legs!
And two eyes that look like cakes!
'Blop bloop', the alien said,
I said it back to him.

'Do you want to come back with me,
After I put the English flag in?'
'Es peas'.

Then I woke up, it was only a dream!

Charlotte Thomas (10)
Eastry CE Primary School

Scary Monster

My name is Eggwardo, I look like a rotten egg,
I've got smelly wings as sharp as daggers,
My teeth are as spiky as shocked maggots,
My house is in Uranus,
Where the rings are two floppy legs.

I am as purple as a plum,
I can pick up five hundred million great whites,
I have three scary eyes
And have sharp pointy ears.

Brandon Crane (9)
Eastry CE Primary School

The Journey To The Moon

A great big whoosh and we're off into the stars,
A zoom and a bang and we're flying past Mars,
The gravity level is very low,
The chairs in the rocket are soft, although
I feel sick as I'm up so high.
Suddenly I go past a huge star. My!
We have a big boom,
We landed on the moon!

Vanessa Burns (9)
Eastry CE Primary School

My Teacher

My teacher is clearly a dream!
We never got thumped on the bum
When we couldn't do an algebra sum.
We never got whacked with the slipper
Even when we started to chatter.
We never got slapped with the cane.
Even if we said school was lame.

We occasionally got told off,
Our punishment was to make the windows sparkle
Just with a piece of old cloth.

The teachers we've had before
Had caned us again and again,
By the end of the year our bottoms were red
And felt like a fire in flame.

This teacher has been the best teacher ever!

Megan Fisher (10)
Kingsdown & Ringwould CEP School

Bernie McMoan

Bernie McMoan,
Lived in a world of his own.
His teachers all thought,
That he could not be taught,
But Bernie McMoan did not mind that,
He just carried on stuffing peas in his hat.

Bernie McMoan,
Lived in a world of his own,
He ate all his books,
And threw food at the cooks,
And then carried on eating the phone.

Bernie McMoan,
Lived in a world of his own,
He kept his thoughts locked away with a key,
So that his happy mind could run free.
But Bernie McMoan,
Lived in a world of his own.

Emily Brookes (10)
Kingsdown & Ringwould CEP School

Green Cow

There once was a cow called Maisy,
Who liked to chew on a daisy
Before they went to bed,
The other cows said,
'What on earth are you doing?'
So they were mooing,
But Maisy was dancing,
What she called prancing,
The night away,
Oh what a beautiful, pure *gold* tray!

Rebecca Stagg (10)
Kingsdown & Ringwould CEP School

Months Of The Year

In January it starts to snow,
In February the cold winds blow,
In March it is the start of spring,
Who knows what April will bring?

May brings flowers in full bloom,
Always June comes much too soon,
July is hot and warm and fun,
In August there is lots of sun.

In September there are apples to eat,
In October it is time to trick or treat,
In November it is firework time,
December brings us Christmas time!

Sarah Carlotti (10)
Kingsdown & Ringwould CEP School

Suspicions

An alien came the other day,
What happened, well I'm going to say.
With hair the colour of underwear,
And cheeks a shade of blue,
It had a thing around its neck,
It was called a nooglenoo.
It had four arms and four legs too,
It's skin looked like something you'd find down the loo.
But my brother said, jumping up with glee,
'It's me he's come for, me, me, me!'
But I didn't believe him you see.
Luckily the alien had come,
Just to say, 'Hello chum!'
Because what I'd always thought is true,
My brother was an alien too!

Charys Dewhurst (10)
Kingsdown & Ringwould CEP School

Spring, Summer, Autumn And Winter

Spring is the best time of year
Because that's when the snowdrops and daffodils appear
You've got the butterflies and caterpillars that come every year
Every day in winter, every time in the year
It will get nearer and nearer to the best part of the year.

Summer can be hot as the season does unfold
Usually the sun shines in the sky big and bold
It's never cold, never ever cold
When the sun in the sky shines big and bold
When the sun shines it makes my day
Because the sun is shining with a smiling, shining face, *hooray!*

Uh-oh, it's that time of year again when the leaves fall
With piles of leaves at the bottom of trees big and tall
They're browny-red and yellow and green
People come to the park and sweep up the leaves
and help make it clean
So say thanks to the people who sweep up our leaves
After watching the children kick about all our leaves.

Hooray, it's that time every year we have snow falling
Everybody loves snow and you're constantly trying to keep the
snowman cooling
You must run inside and ask for buttons, a carrot, hat and scarf.
It's snowball time and everyone is trying to hit the others
and hear them laugh
Uh-oh, everyone's parents are coming to bring us in
from the cold air,
But we say, 'No, please no, we love it out here!'
And they say, 'Well it's time for bed,
Come on up to bed with a hot water bottle and a cup of
cocoa instead.'

Isabel Castle (10)
Kingsdown & Ringwould CEP School

Looking Round Schools

Oh what are the tools,
For looking round schools,
To me it brings a headache.
The staff look grumpy,
The teachers are frumpy,
Oh what a decision to make!

Looking round the maths rooms,
Smelling like rats' tombs,
To me it brings a headache.
The food looks all yucky,
The pupils all mucky,
Oh what a decision to make!

The homework looks tricky,
The teachers are picky,
To me it brings a headache.
The playground looks small,
The hall looks tall,
Oh what a decision to make!

The art room looks great,
The English I hate,
To me it brings a headache.
Parents are worried,
Teachers are hurried,
Oh what a decision to make!

The books are dusty,
The goalposts rusty,
To me it brings a headache.
How can I know,
Where I should go?
Oh what decision to make.

Tabitha Shepherd (10)
Kingsdown & Ringwould CEP School

My Trip To The Park

I ride up to the park with my friends
We swing on the swings as high as the sky,
Holding as tight as ever,
We come back down to find it rains.

We skip to the equipment
And swing around and around on the turning log,
Gripping as hard as we can,
Falling down to find the sun.

We fly to the play house,
And climb up on the roof,
Grasping to the beginning of a new planet,
Sliding down to find the snow.

I ride home with my friends,
Riding through a dark, winding pathway
Finally I get home and find my mum and dad
I have done my dare!

Amy Brown (10)
Kingsdown & Ringwould CEP School

Bike Ride

We go on a bike ride down the hills, over the bumps.
The wind blowing in our faces, sending tears down our faces.
Me and my brother have loads of races.

Trees and bushes go rushing by
Up and down the country lanes we ride,
All the family in a line.

We stop and have a little rest,
Then back in the saddle because homeward bound is best.

Tara Hodgkins (10)
Kingsdown & Ringwould CEP School

My Best Friend

My best friend is called Amy Brown
When we are together I never feel down

She makes me laugh until I cry
To be her best friend, I never have to try

She's cool and funny and kind to me
Without my best friend I don't know where I'd be

We sit together in our class
And eat our lunch together on the grass

After school when I go to her house
Sometimes she's as quiet as a mouse

But when we play on the trampoline
We bounce so high she starts to scream

When I sleep there overnight
We chat and giggle until it's light

When we're together I never need to frown
Because she's my best friend, Amy Brown.

Alannah Taylor (10)
Kingsdown & Ringwould CEP School

Growing Up

When I was a baby I couldn't wait
To be tall like my mum and dad.
I had my patchwork coat but I just couldn't reach
The tops of the trees.
As I grew and grew I could reach higher and higher.
Now I am all grown-up and I can eat the tender little shoots
At the top of the trees.
Now I am a beautiful giraffe, just like my mum and dad.

Amy Miller (10)
Kingsdown & Ringwould CEP School

Impatience

I'm sitting in my classroom,
I've been here all day,
Tick-tock, tick-tock,
I'm confused and bored
And I just want to play,
Tick-tock, tick-tock,
The letters and the numbers
Seem to wriggle round the page,
Tick-tock, tick-tock,
I feel like an animal
Trapped in a cage,
Tick-tock, tick-tock,
My brow begins to sweat
As the teacher walks past,
Tick-tock, tick-tock,
She says the test's over,
Hooray! At last!

Jessica Henry (10)
Kingsdown & Ringwould CEP School

My Cat

I have a kitten that is called Button
He stretches like Mum
He miaows a lot of times
He miaows because he wants to go outside
Also he miaows because he does not have any food
He scratches on the pillows and clothes
He jumps around a lot
He runs fast around the garden
He follows Mum around
And he also scratches my bed and Mum and Dad's bed.

Micheal Wright (10)
Kingsdown & Ringwould CEP School

Big School Bully

There once was a girl called Julie,
Who was the big school bully!
She would tease the little ones,
Pull their hair and bite their thumbs.
There once was a boy called Joey,
Who said, 'No, no, no. Noey!'
He went to tell their headmaster
Who then burst out with laughter,
'What do you mean, our pupils are the best,
They certainly beat all the rest.'
Joey then told his mum and dad,
That the bully was very bad.
They all went to school, the next day
And got the bully out of the way.

So don't let yourself get bullied,
And *don't* turn into one like Julie!

Ellenor Hadlow (10)
Kingsdown & Ringwould CEP School

Luie And Mr Koat

There once was a man called Luie
Who was absolutely screwy
He earned his money
By being funny
That silly old man called Luie.

There once was a man called Mr Koat
Whatever he did he stayed on the boat
In the month of May
He fished every day
That silly man called Mr Koat.

Roman Gronkowski (11)
Kingsdown & Ringwould CEP School

Hallowe'en

There are sweets to eat and apples to bite
On this cold and chilly October night

Where the shadows of witches are there on the moon
And all sorts of ghosts will be out there soon

Werewolves howling and goblins screaming
Add to the terror of children dreaming

By the blazing fire in a comfy home
We're safe at last from the creatures who roam.

William Sparrow (10)
Kingsdown & Ringwould CEP School

Nice Little Spider

Nice little spider on the wall,
Nice little spider had a great fall,
Nice little spider banged his head,
Poor little spider, sadly dead.

Jennifer Trower (10)
Kingsdown & Ringwould CEP School

Grunion Forest

Wibbley, gibbley bugs come from Grunion Forest.
Maggots, worms and spiders crawl out of the princess' turrets,
Sickening creatures, from beyond the grave, slither
                                        to Grunion Forest.
But none match the queen of filth and grime,
But you only see her there when the great moon shines.
So come creatures, come, think twice before you enter.

Mollie Letheren-Smith (10)
Kingsdown & Ringwould CEP School

Born To Be Green

I support Plymouth,
The team who plays in green,
Supporting from the Devonport end,
The finest I've ever seen.

I think the ground is great,
My stomach turns standing at the gate,
You should hear the rumble when they score a goal,
They could probably hear the cheer in the North Pole.

Paul Wotton is the captain of the team,
When things go wrong he gets really mean,
Fists go flying through the air,
The ref looks at them all in despair.

With only five minutes left to play,
It looks like you've given it all away,
Come on Plymouth, don't let us down,
You might just win with a frown.

Jack Mashford (10)
Kingsdown & Ringwould CEP School

Lego

These things make some people happy:
Eclipse of the sun, the moon in a dark sky,
Mountains in a sunset, clear seas with tropical fishes.

But this is what makes me happy - Lego!
Lego, Lego, Batman and Star Wars,
Lego City, Rescue too,
Lego boats, and Lego castles,
Lego pirates and disasters.
Making models is great fun
So is playing with them when they're done!

Andrew White (10)
Kingsdown & Ringwould CEP School

I'd Love A Cat

I'd love a cat,
I'd put it in a funny hat.
I'd like a cat that was really soft,
I'd keep it in the loft.
I'd like to watch it lick its paws,
I'd hope it hasn't got sharp claws.
I'd like a cat with emerald eyes,
I'd find it funny if it ate mince pies.
I'd wish it was black,
Like coal in a sack.
I'd like a cat with a long tail,
That's the cat in the sale.

Chloe Brown (10)
Kingsdown & Ringwould CEP School

Love Poem

Love is pink, like the bits that come out of our hearts.
It sounds like the beauty of music.
You can see it when it's Valentine's Day.
It reminds me of my boyfriend.
It feels like I am cared for and loved.

Paige Garrett (8)
Offham CP School

Laughter

Laughter is yellow like happiness in my dreams.
It sounds like you're flying in a cloud.
You can see it when a smile, giggle and a laugh appears.

Laughter reminds me of children playing happily in the sun.
It makes me feel happy and joyful.

Stanley Draper (8)
Offham CP School

Love

Love is pink like the petals of a rose.
It sounds like beautiful music.
You can see it when the sun is setting.
It reminds me of my best friend
It makes me feel happy.

Joshua Burford (8)
Offham CP School

The Flow Of Happiness

Happiness is golden like the sun up in the sky,
It sounds like the tinkle of a bell,
Happiness rises when Saturday dawns,
The shine of gold reminds me of the joy of happiness,
Happiness makes me feel sunny and joyful.

The feeling of happiness runs through my blood,
Happiness dancers dance out of the sky,
The boat of joy runs out of the harbour,
Happiness flows, flows away,
Until the light has gone.

Clarissa Price (10)
Offham CP School

Love

Love is pink like the pinkest, best doll.
It sounds like a nice rhythm of music.
You can see it when it's Valentine's Day.
Love reminds me of my family.
It makes me feel happy.

Katrine Khomitch (8)
Offham CP School

Anger

Anger is red like the face of my mum when she's angry.
It sounds like her face splitting apart.
It looks like a tiny piece of thread.
Anger reminds me of cars crashing.
It makes me feel like my head has dropped off,
Because I screamed too much!

James Turner (8)
Offham CP School

Anger

Anger is red like a scorpion in the hot Sahara desert.
It sounds like you're getting steamy.

You can see it when someone is about to stamp their heavy feet,
Like an angry elephant.
It looks like the whole world is about to have the biggest explosion.

Anger reminds me of your face, steaming red,
Like an extremely hot barbecue.

It makes me feel like people are putting explosives in my head.

Elizabeth Berman (8)
Offham CP School

Anger

Anger is red like the reddest, most fiery volcano exploding.
It sounds like a big bang.

You can see it when you stamp your feet,
Scream like a dinosaur and you're about to explode.

Anger reminds me of the roof blowing off.
It makes me feel horrible and flaming hot inside.

Josh Haselden (8)
Offham CP School

Fear

Fear is grey like the rainy clouds.
It sounds like your roof has been taken off.
You can see it when my eyes widen with horror.

It reminds me of storm clouds starting to begin.
It makes me feel scared with fear in my body.

Hanah Ahmed (8)
Offham CP School

Fear

Fear is blue like the bluest sky that birds can fly in.
It sounds like a bear's tummy rumbling from hunger.
You can see it when my eyes begin to widen and fill with tears.
Fear reminds me of the poorest of all things
In pain and bursting into pools of tears.
It makes me feel like sad tears, with annoying pains.

Lucy Christmas (8)
Offham CP School

Fear

Fear is blue like the sea crashing against the rocks.
It sounds like the wind blowing hard against the clouds.
You can see it's twirling with slightly cold wind.
Fear reminds me of great twirling rain from the cold air.
It makes me feel like curving back in horror.

Kathryn Parker (8)
Offham CP School

Fear

Fear is grey like the meanest blowing rain cloud, too near.
It sounds like wind blowing nearer and right here.
You can see it when my body seems to make
a tiny wet thing blowing down my cheek; a tear.
Fear reminds me of when I was in a terrible storm.
It makes me feel like running away without looking back,
but my legs are just too warm.

Melissa Seabrook (8)
Offham CP School

Fear

Fear is grey like the white fierce wind.
It sounds like very windy clouds passing by on a dull, windy day.
You can see it when I start dropping down my arms and screaming
like I've been robbed!
Fear reminds me of a hamster running away madly.
It makes me feel like nobody or nothing likes me, and a storm is
blowing over me.

Erin Baker (8)
Offham CP School

Laughter

Laughter is yellow like the happiness in my dreams.
It sounds like you're flying in a hot air balloon.
You can see it when you have a smile, a giggle and then
laughter appears.
Laughter reminds me of children playing happily in the sun.
It makes me feel like playing in a dream cave
with the sun shining through.

Jacob Hancock (8)
Offham CP School

Happiness

Happiness is pink like the love and joy inside everyone.
It sounds like children laughing and playing happily, all together.
You see it when two eyes meet and end up skipping merrily
down the road.
It reminds you of your first ever birthday.
It makes you feel like the luckiest kid in the world!

Benjamin Chapman (11)
Offham CP School

Laughter

Laughter is yellow like the bright yellow sun.
It sounds like children playing under the sun.
You can see it when you put that big smile
on your face like the sun beaming its flames.
Laughter reminds me of hot, sunny, summer days.
It makes me feel like I am going to go on to
a nice, hot, relaxing beach.

Elynor Alderton (8)
Offham CP School

Happiness

Happiness is yellow like the yellow sun.
It sounds like people laughing.
You can see it whenever you want to.
Happiness reminds me of playing in the park with my friends.
It makes me feel delightful and cheerful.

Dan Chapman (8)
Offham CP School

Happiness

Happiness is yellow like the sunniest of days.
It sounds like laughter.
You can see it when someone is falling over with the giggles.
Happiness reminds me of Christmas Day.
It makes me feel happy, sleepy and comfy.

Caitlin Foxell (8)
Offham CP School

Temperature

Heat
Heat is red, the colour of hot,
Heat annoys a baby, struggling in its cot.
Heat engulfs the African plains,
Heat's arch enemy is definitely the rain.
Heat loves fire, destroying everything in its path,
Heat helps the newborn calf.

Cold
Cold is gloomy grey, the colour of mist on a winter's day,
Cold disappears by the end of May,
Cold is the source of dreaded frostbite,
Cold engulfs Antarctica, nothing but white,
Cold is friendly to penguins and seals,
Cold makes you ill, so have a few nice hot meals!

Jack Davis (11)
Offham CP School

Happiness

Happiness is green like the grass shining in the sun.
It sounds like twinkling chimes.
You can see it when it is in a lovely green, rich garden.
Happiness reminds me of laughter at Christmas.
It makes me feel really cheerful and happy.

Jack Brown (8)
Offham CP School

Family Pets

I have a pet frog,
Who lives in a log,
And he's rather fond
Of my garden pond.

My brother has a hen,
She lives in her pen,
She likes to eat bugs
And is mad about slugs.

My dad has a snail,
Who loves curly kale,
He sits in Dad's hair
And goes to sleep there!

My mum has a budgie
And she's very pudgy,
She eats too much pie,
And we think that is why!

Vivien Hadlow (10)
Offham CP School

Anger

Anger is like a crimson tornado,
Like the blood of a Roman foe.
It grabs all the happiness from you,
And holds onto you like superglue.

It sounds like the screaming girl of the night,
It tries to suffocate you by coming without sight.
You can see it when the werewolves are howling with rage,
It's like it's escaped the Devil's cage.

Anger reminds you of unimaginable hate,
It makes you feel like you'll never reach Heaven's gates,
It makes you feel like a self-centred devil.
For rage it makes you feel off the level.

Oliver Haselden (11)
Offham CP School

Love

Love is crimson like the burning glow in the darkness,
Love sounds like beating drums humming in the distance.
You can see love in the most unlikely places,
In a church, in a restaurant, in the cinema, anywhere it's possible.
Love reminds me of joy and laughter spreading everywhere.
Love makes me feel like an angel on my way to Heaven.

Yasmin-Hanna Ryan (10)
Offham CP School

Love

Love is endless at first meeting,
Love is joyful and you can never get to sleep,
Love can be depressing and can get into a mess,
Love can lead into an antagonising argument,
Love is as beautiful as a rose.
When the red Devil is ready to kill
It normally leaves people in tears of sadness.

Jack Ball (10)
Offham CP School

Happiness

Happiness is orange,
Like the sun on a Saturday morning,
It sounds like the laughter of children playing,
You can see it when Saturday dawns.
Happiness reminds me of children giggling,
Laughing on the green, green grass,
It makes me feel as if birds are singing outside
My window, like an orchestra.

Maxim Gorham (10)
Offham CP School

My Magic Box

(Based on 'Magic Box' by Kit Wright)

I would put in my magic box . . .
A curl of the football hitting the net
A big, fluffy dog jumping through a field.
Creamy chocolate melting in my mouth.

I would put in my magic box . . .
The delicious smell of hot chocolate,
A carpet of snow,
Barking dogs and quacking ducks.

I would put in my magic box . . .
Liverpool winning the Premiership,
Chelsea getting relegated,
The lovely whoosh of the sea.

I would put in my magic box . . .
No vicious dinosaurs,
A pair of Lacoste shoes,
And an Xbox 360.

Danny Green-Ryan (10)
Our Lady of Hartley RC Primary School

Autumn

A pples in orchards growing, yellow, red and green,
U nder branches brown and very lean.
T rees so bare they're practically naked,
U nder trees the leaves are red.
M oles hibernating far below the ground,
N ow winter's coming happiness all around!

R ed leaves falling from trees to the ground.
E verywhere the trunks of oaks are standing around,
D own by the river conkers I've found!

Liam Spurin (10)
Our Lady of Hartley RC Primary School

My Magical World

When I was a child
I went absolutely wild,
Making lots of exciting rides
Then I would whizz down slides!

I went absolutely bonkers
When I was playing conkers!
I dressed up as Superman
And sometimes got a van.

I read brilliant books
And tried to cook.
I made the best tents
But not out of cement.

Then at the end of the day
I had to pack away,
Then I had to go to sleep
And I couldn't play and leap.

Zac Maidment (10)
Our Lady of Hartley RC Primary School

Lotty

Is there such a thing as the Easter bunny?
Is Father Christmas really funny?
Is my dad good at jokes?
My mum talks to all the blokes.

Are there such things as slugs and snails?
Are there such things as dolphins and whales?
Are there such things as cats and dogs?
Are there such things as logs and frogs?

Am I a girl or a boy?
Wherever I go I bring my toy.
When I was born my mum called me Lotty
And when I was one I learnt to use the potty.

Lara Paton (9)
Our Lady of Hartley RC Primary School

The Seasons Of The Year

Spring is when the flowers bud
And the leaves are glowing green
And the weather's getting warm
And I am going to love it.

Summer is when the weather's great
And the sun is out
And the holidays are coming
And I can play outside.

Autumn's when the leaves change colour
And the weather's getting cold
And the sun has gone away
And the leaves are off the trees.

Winter's when the snow is out,
The Christmas trees are up
And the angels are on the top,
Lots of pretty colours.

Megan Skey (9)
Our Lady of Hartley RC Primary School

When I Was A Child

When I was a child, I went wild
Mind you I was a little child,
Jumping in the garden like I was in the woods
While I was wearing two hoods.

Like a lion in the jungle,
I wouldn't roar but I might mumble,
Like a monkey in a tree
Saying, 'Oh ha, he, he.'

If I was an animal,
I would be a dog barking
Or a warthog, barking at the moon,
Saying, 'See you soon.'

Lewis Wright (10)
Our Lady of Hartley RC Primary School

My Super Box
(Based on 'Magic Box' by Kit Wright)

I will put in my box . . .
A gust of wind from the biggest tornado,
A splinter of wood from Jesus' cross,
A lightsaber used by a Jedi.

I will put in my box . . .
A lump of tank from Operation Torch,
A pistol from the D-Day landings,
A chip of tile from Churchill's porch.

I will put in my box . . .
A gold pot from a leprechaun,
The cry of the banshee,
A fairy darting across a fairy glade.

My box is made of gold and sapphire,
Tank wheels and a bomb.
And if you want to find it your search will be quite long.

Padraig Flaherty (10)
Our Lady of Hartley RC Primary School

Hello Autumn

Hello autumn,
Goodbye flowers,
Here come bad showers.

Walking down the crispy road,
Some of the red is showed,
In the sun or in the rain,
All year round it is a pain.

The leaves are dead and the trees are bare
It's really not fair,
Leaf fights are so much fun,
Especially when you get a cream bun!

Katie McCaughey (10)
Our Lady of Hartley RC Primary School

Fifteen Rats

Fifteen rats were gathered in a mound,
Sniffling and snuffling in the sewer,
But one got washed away in a drain,
Then there were fourteen.

Fourteen rats gathered in a mound,
Sniffling and snuffling for cheese,
Three got caught in a rat trap,
Then there were eleven.

Eleven rats were gathered in a mound,
Sniffing and snuffling in a cottage,
Five got caught and thrown into a field,
Then there were six.

Six rats were gathered in a mound,
Sniffling and snuffling in the road,
Five got squashed by a motor car,
And then there was one.

One rat was on his own,
Looking for a friend to play,
A cat came and gobbled him up,
And then there were none!

Jeffrey Horscroft (11)
Our Lady of Hartley RC Primary School

School Rules

Do not push
Do not rush
Do not run in class

Have kind hands and feet
Be polite to all you meet
Make sure you wash your hands

Otherwise you will get detention!

Sarah Day (9)
Our Lady of Hartley RC Primary School

Do Fish?

Do fish,
Do swordfish really fight with swords?
Do flying fish really fly?
Do clownfish really clown around?
Deep down there!

Do fish,
Do anglerfish go angling?
Do weaver fish weave jumpers for their young?
Do angelfish really live up to their name?
Deep down there!

Do fish,
Do whales wail every night and day?
Do sole fish look after the souls of the dead?
Do octopuses keep pussycats?
Deep down there!

Do fish,
Do apollo sharks have regular trips to the moon?
Does a balloon molly blow up like a balloon?
Do blue-faced discus fish enter into the Olympics?
Deep down there!

Do fish,
Does a fire mouth fish really breathe fire?
Does a big jewel-faced fish wear lots of jewels?
Does a pink kisser fish go kissing all the boys?
Deep down there!

Eleanor Sparling (11)
Our Lady of Hartley RC Primary School

Shark!

S harp teeth
H orrible and cruel
A cts fast
R eef dweller
K ing of the fish!

Thomas Gibbins
Our Lady of Hartley RC Primary School

My Little Box

(Based on 'Magic Box' by Kit Wright)

I will put in my little box . . .
Two tons of burning magma from a volcano,
A piece of horn from a rhino's head,
A boxing kangaroo from Australia.

I will put in my little box . . .
a baby that talks and an adult that mumbles,
a spot from a cheetah's skin,
a roaring tiger fish and a swimming tiger.

I will put in my little box . . .
a piece of tentacle from a Kraken,
a snowball from Mount Everest,
a tiny little cloud which I could ride on.

My box has a gold lining with a . . .
forcefield around it and it is
made out of titanium
and it is well protected.

I shall keep it with me until
new adventures come
and some unusual and beautiful things,
then I will get my box.

Juan Miguel Cabling (10)
Our Lady of Hartley RC Primary School

Sweets

S weets are fabulous,
W e eat them sometimes.
E at candy, chocolate,
E at, munch, chew.
T aste amazing, great!
S weets are gorgeous.

Ella Cooper (8)
Our Lady of Hartley RC Primary School

My Magic Box

(Based on 'Magic Box' by Kit Wright)

I will put in the box . . .
The smell of red roses,
Scissors that can write,
Pencils that can cut!

I will put in the box . . .
Fish with fur,
Kittens with gills,
A tree with £20 notes on it.

I will put in the box . . .
Milky pure chocolate that melts on your tongue,
Pit-a-pat, pit-a-pat, rainfalls,
Velvety smooth hot chocolate.

I will put in the box . . .
Clear blue water that sparkles in the sun,
Clouds of fluff,
Wool of sheep.

Alice Steingass (10)
Our Lady of Hartley RC Primary School

Me And My Family

Was it true that maybe,
My mum would have a baby,
When my mum changed my nappy,
My dad was very happy!

When I was two,
I learnt to tie my shoe.
When I took off my diaper,
I went very hyper!

When I started school,
I was really quite small.
When I was seven,
My nana went to Heaven!

Hannah Gillespie (9)
Our Lady of Hartley RC Primary School

I Love Guinea Pigs

Do you like guinea pigs with their jelly feet?
I've got guinea pigs don't you think they are sweet?
One little guinea pig is a little cheeky thing,
When I give her a treat, oh how she wants to sing.

Don't you think they are sweet?
Squeak, squeak, when they want some food,
Sometimes they squeak so much it gets rude,
Jump, jump, jump, when they are happy with a smile,
Slide! Slide! When they walk on a glass tile.

Don't you think they are sweet?
Once they get to know you they start to lick,
Even if your skin is really rough and thick,
My little guinea pigs lick so much,
It's much worse than a human touch.

Don't you think they are sweet?
I love them so much I get my guinea pigs out every day.
We both cry when they have to go away.
Six girls, no boys.
You have to treat them better than six toys.

Billy Goldsmith (10)
Our Lady of Hartley RC Primary School

Football

F un to watch and fun to play
O xford have a free kick because of an offside
O fficials are watching the game
T errific teams playing
B uying players
A ll the teams have amazing attackers
L ost some players got some new but
L ost because of the new players!

Michael Gardiner (9)
Our Lady of Hartley RC Primary School

Different People

People around us are never the same,
You get people who like different things,
He likes rock CDs and she likes rings.

People around us are never the same,
You get people who are unique,
They are African and he is Sikh.

People around us are never the same,
You get people who look alike,
But he is Tom and he is Mike.

People around us are never the same,
You get people who act differently,
Like they are silly and she acts sensibly.

People around us are never the same,
You get people with a different attitude,
She's lazy and he's in a healthy mood.

So we should all thank
God for making us different!

Dheelan Sydamah (10)
Our Lady of Hartley RC Primary School

Chelsea

C aptain being cheered
H ome team scores a goal
E xcited crowd cheering us to win
L ampard scoring all the goals
S lide-tackling around the leg
E verybody shouting, *'Chelsea!'*
A win for Chelsea.

Catherine Rye (8)
Our Lady of Hartley RC Primary School

Horses

Horses, horses
Good and bad,
Some are happy and some are sad.

Some are good
And don't need training,
They even obey you when it's raining.

Horses, horses
Good and bad,
Some are happy and some are sad.

Some are bad
They go on all day,
Sometimes they're naughty straight away.

Horses, horses
Good and bad,
Some are happy and some are sad.

Some are happy
They laugh and play,
They're always happy, anyway.

Horses, horses
Good and bad,
Some are happy and some are sad.

Some are sad
They go away,
They never ever do what you say.

Horses

Zofia Gawor (10)
Our Lady of Hartley RC Primary School

A Season Of Our Life

Autumn, just another season of our life,
The wind blows, like a whetted knife.
All the leaves float to the ground,
They gently hit without a sound.

Autumn, just another season of the year,
Summer is just about to jump off a cliff,
Harvest, a ceremony of food,
You won't be in an angry mood.

Autumn, just another season of celebration,
All over the nation,
There's Bonfire Night,
And Hallowe'en, you get a fright.

Autumn, just another season of our life,
No more spring cleaning for anyone's wife.
Squirrels stealing nuts,
And running to their huts.

Charlie Scott Flint (10)
Our Lady of Hartley RC Primary School

Funny Animals

Cats and rats and blind little bats,
Cows and horses,
Stags charge with forces.

Lousy dogs lay on logs,
Rabbits and their bunnies
Hop around quite funny.

Tigers and lions fight,
They fight until night

There are so many animals everywhere,
I forgot to tell you about the grizzly bear!

Ella Marriner (10)
Our Lady of Hartley RC Primary School

Music

Do you like music?

There's all different types of music,
If you've just started to like it,
You'll start off with pop,
And move on to rock.

Do you like music?

You may like funk,
And not like punk,
When you're fixing a tap,
You're listening to rap.

Do you like music?

You smell a pong,
While listening to a song!
You're at a concert with DJ Joe,
After five minutes he's got to go.

Do you like music?

Eminem's retiring,
You're gonna fire him,
You're listening to Beastie Boys,
Whilst playing with baby toys.

Do you like music?

You're going to see Black-Eyed Peas,
With a new pair of knees!
You like singing blues,
But after you need lots of clues.

Do you like music?

You're listening to legends,
It might be fun,
Now you like music,
You don't need a gun!

Henry Goodwin (10)
Our Lady of Hartley RC Primary School

Gymnastics

Gymnastics is the best!
Learn lots of things like,
Cartwheels, handstands, crabs and splits,
Gymnastics is the best!

Gymnastics is the best!
Jumping on the trampoline,
Swinging on the bars,
Gymnastics is the best!

Gymnastics is the best!
Doing flips, backward flips,
Never forgetting forward flips,
Gymnastics is the best!

Gymnastics is the best!
Now doing cartwheels into splits,
And handstands into crab,
Gymnastics is the best!

Gymnastics is the best!
Doing things you couldn't do,
That now you're the best of all of it,
Gymnastics is the best!

Gymnastics is the best!
As far as you can see,
Come along and join,
Gymnastics is the *best*!

Maria Gemmell (10)
Our Lady of Hartley RC Primary School

Glamorous City

What are you able to do with your head?
Don't stay in bed,
Dressing up and performing shows,
Wearing pretty little bows!

Cavorting round and round,
Hopscotch without a sound!
Cushions thrown up into the sky,
Me being shy.

Making shadows on the wall,
Catching a squashy ball,
Falling over is not the best,
Don't even rest!

Build a house in your room,
A chimney using a broom!
Jumping, jumping up and down,
Your hands swinging round!

Flying through the door,
And missing Mrs Moore,
Eating chocolate cake,
The one you always bake.

Remembering all you can,
You and Sam,
Wish you were there,
Playing with the bear!

Ella Shire (10)
Our Lady of Hartley RC Primary School

Football Mad

Football is the best sport
It is the greatest
Most people are football crazy
And some hate it

Girls especially don't like it
But some women do
The reason that some like football
Because there is ladies' football too

Rotherham are rubbish
Chelsea are the best
Man United are great
But do Arsenal need to improve?

So if you like footy
You are great
But remember this all the time
Football is the best sport.

James Gilhooly (9)
Our Lady of Hartley RC Primary School

Dog Tale

Springer spaniel sniffing out trouble,
Helping people trapped in a cave, trapped under rocks,
Helping the army day and night,
Leaving their sides just to help, day and night.

King Charles spaniel, loyal to the King.
Listening to the King when he needs someone to talk to.

Cocker spaniel last of the spaniel family,
See its glowing eyes at night.
Keep an eye on your dog as you watch it jumping,
Through the fields, jumping through the moonlight sky.
Shih-tzu, Shih-tzu, walking at night,
Sometimes people give it a big fright,
Walking across the dark misty night, know it has might.

Aaron Carlse (10)
Our Lady of Hartley RC Primary School

The Magic Box

(Based on 'Magic Box' by Kit Wright)

I will put into the box . . .
The cold of the northern wind
The heat of the southern sun,
And a vast carpet of snow.

I will put into the box . . .
A wave from the Caribbean sea,
A cosy pub in the country,
And a long-lost ancient animal.

I will put into the box . . .
The smell of freshly mown grass,
The first touch of a newborn baby,
And the ancient voice of a long-lost soul.

My box is made from the sun and stars,
Decorated with the moons and planets,
The key is made of solid gold.

I will surf on a great wave,
And drive in my flashy car,
In my huge, sparkly magic box.

Joshua Price (10)
Our Lady of Hartley RC Primary School

Football

F ootball is the most popular sport in the world
O ur country is very good at it
O ur school has football training after school
T op clubs are very popular and some are not
B olton, Birmingham and Blackburn are not so popular
A nd Arsenal and Argentina are very popular
L ucky Chelsea won the Premiership
L ong ago Liverpool were the best.

Joe Scott (10)
Our Lady of Hartley RC Primary School

Dancing

What dancing do I like?

Ballet is smooth,
Petite, quiet and fun,
I like the mimes best!

What dancing do I like?

Tap is snazzy,
Loud, soundful, fun,
I like all bits of tap!

What dancing do I like?

Ballroom is fun,
Cha-cha, samba, tango,
I like jive best!

What dancing do I like?

Jazz is funky,
Classy, jazzy, fun,
I like the shaking best!

When I grow up
I want to be a
Dancing queen!

Alice Belcher (10)
Our Lady of Hartley RC Primary School

My Magic Box

(Based on 'Magic Box' by Kit Wright)

I will put into my box . . .
The great teeth of the sabre-tooth tiger,
And a mine full of gold,
The wonderful taste of mint.

I will put into my box . . .
All the dinosaurs from prehistoric times,
And an eclipse every week,
The roar of a dragon in the morning sun.

I will put into my box . . .
A thousand greetings, all in different languages,
Six minds to think for me,
A great moon made of cheese.

My box will be fashioned with dragon scales,
Rubies and emeralds, even pure gold edges,
And the joints will be made of silver bullets.

I shall journey in my box
Finding all new things for me,
Then on to dangerous adventures,
Things like volcanoes burning red.

Conor Moody (10)
Our Lady of Hartley RC Primary School

My Magic Box

(Based on 'Magic Box' by Kit Wright)

I will put in my box . . .
Smoke from the Fire of London,
Hair from a mountain goat's head,
A chocolate banana, straight off the barbecue.

I will put in my box . . .
A brain that cuts and scissors that think,
Fishes that breathed fire and dragons that swim,
Rain as hot as the sun and freezing cold sunshine.

I will put in my box . . .
A bullet from a sniper's rifle,
A bullet from a shotgun,
And a rocket from a rocket launcher coming after me!

I will put in my box . . .
The touch of a dragon scale,
The touch of an electric eel,
And the touch of a baby.

My box will be fashioned with swords and shields,
Jewels in the corner and armour on the inside protecting my box.

Calum Cook (11)
Our Lady of Hartley RC Primary School

Cheeky Cheetah

I am a cheeky cheetah,
I can see slimy bugs,
I can hear elephants,
I can smell my dinner,
My lovely, lovely dinner,
I can live in my foggy cave,
I can go and get my dinner.

Imogen Menage
Our Lady of Hartley RC Primary School

Once Upon A Dream

My first dream,
On that summer night,
Cinderella was there looking in my eyes,
With her princess friends.
Once upon a dream!

With a kiss on the cheek,
From a boy that I meet.
Once upon a dream!

My second dream,
I'm going to Hollywood,
To be a superstar,

Make-up in my bedroom,
Make-up everywhere.
Once upon a dream!

The prince and princess,
At the top of the tower.
Once upon a dream!

My final dream,
The queen and the king,
In the middle of Rome,
In the fashion shops,
Will spend, spend, spend.
Once upon a dream!

Twinkle, twinkle,
Said Tinkerbell.
Once upon a dream!

Kate Elizabeth Evans (10)
Our Lady of Hartley RC Primary School

Imaginary City

What do you think of in your mind,
Whether in front or behind?
Bring your friends and come and play with me,
Find out what you can see . . .
Let's play princesses and army,
For tea we can have salami!
Climb up trees, jump on a bed,
'Mind, you're on Ned's head!'

Let's draw pictures and paint them too,
After we can play hide-and-seek, *boo.*
Mum and Dad are coming to play,
'Come on Mum, this way!'

Don't tease the dog dear, she is only small,
Dad look, she likes the ball!
Let's carry on climbing trees,
'Not in that one, there's lots of bees!'

Goodbye for now, no more play,
We have been doing it all day!
We need to tidy the games away,
'That is my one, hey!'

Kira Ratcliffe (10)
Our Lady of Hartley RC Primary School

My House

In my house
I see dogs playing
With their toys.
When I play football
I see my brother William playing too.
Oh no! Not Jammed.
I smell my dinner,
Hooray!

Matthew Steingass (8)
Our Lady of Hartley RC Primary School

Guinea Pigs

Guinea pigs are cute
And eat lots of fruit!
I love guinea pigs,
They are so cute!

My one's very squeaky
And also very cheeky,
I love guinea pigs,
They are so cute!

It makes me cheerful,
Life is never dull,
I love guinea pigs,
They are so cute!

They're very friendly
And they hate jelly!
I love guinea pigs,
They are so cute!

They have a lot of fur
And they can purr.
I love guinea pigs,
They are so cute!

They like lots of food
And they can be very rude,
I love guinea pigs,
They are so cute!

Do you like guinea pigs?
They are so cute!

You must like guinea pigs now,
They're extremely cute!

George Goldsmith (10)
Our Lady of Hartley RC Primary School

The Little Old Man From Strawberrydale

There once was a man from Strawberrydale
He loved his pet dragon and he loved his pet whale
One day he was walking and it started to hail
He sneaked into a house and ran off with some ale
When the housemaid caught up with him she plucked off
his tail (he had a tail?)

He came back with armour, an axe and a bear
He came back with blingage, high heels and no hair
The housemaid saw this and it gave her a scare
She was very frightened, so she phoned up the mayor
The mayor of the town, he was Tony Blair
He answered the phone and shouted, 'Who's there?'

She told him what had happened when the bear broke down the door
He told her what he'd do, he'd summon the wild boar
The bear ran into the room and she dived onto the floor
The bear tried to take a bite at her, it would kill her for sure!
Then, in ran the old man with the axe, knowing there would be gore
The wild boar then rushed in and charged them more and more

The old man ran outside, called his dragon and flew away
The dragon was out of breath and crash-landed in some hay
And unless he's healed all his broken bones, he'll still be there today.

Robert Tucker (10)
Our Lady of Hartley RC Primary School

Autumn Days

Autumn has come and summer has gone.
Underneath spiky shells lay gleaming conkers to sell.
The woods full of bare trees where leaves have fell.
Underneath carpets of leaves lay damp paths made of stone.
Meeting new colours of leaves golden, red, yellow, brown!
Night becomes dark as autumn has come!

Lucy-Anna Littlefield (10)
Our Lady of Hartley RC Primary School

The Stables

My favourite place to be is the stables.
When I stand in a stable I smell damp straw
And the smell of hay.
When I'm outside I can hear cars,
Birds tweeting and children talking.
When I stand in one place
I can feel the coldness on my face
Making my nose all red with coldness.
I can feel hard stones.
I can feel the softness of the pony's coat.
I can taste the salted air all around me.
I can taste little bits of hay.
I can see trees and stables and mud.
I can see the moon going down.
But before we go I just want to tell you,
When you're down with the ponies
It reminds me how cute ponies can be.

Abigail Keenan (7)
Our Lady of Hartley RC Primary School

Dragons

When I am in the world of dragons
I see the dragons fighting
And the flames coming from their mouths.

I smell the smoke from the flames,
I smell the meat from when
The dragons have been eating.

I hear the dragons' footsteps
I hear the dragons roar very loudly.

I can jump on a dragon's back
And fly away.

Megan Penny (7)
Our Lady of Hartley RC Primary School

Little Bo-Peep Lost Her Sheep

'Have any of you seen my sheep?'
Asked confused Little Bo-Peep.
'Nope, I haven't,' said Cinderella
Cleaning the floor in the dark, dark cellar.

'Have any of you seen my sheep?'
Asked the out-of-breath Little Bo-Peep.
'No, we haven't,' said Jack and Jill
Who were eating chocolate on the hill.

'Have any of you seen my sheep?'
Asked the tired Little Bo-Peep.
'No, I haven't,' said the wicked witch
Who'd been stuck in the prickly ditch.

'Have any of you seen my sheep?'
Asked annoyed Little Bo-Peep.
'Nope, I haven't,' said Baby Bear
Who'd finished his porridge and rotten black pear.

'Have any of you seen my sheep?'
Asked poor Little Bo-Peep.
'Nope, I haven't,' said Little Miss Muffet
Checking, before she sat on a tuffet.

'What shall do? I've lost my sheep,'
Said the miserable Little Bo-Peep.
'Baa,' came a voice from behind a castle,
It was Bo's sheep inside a parcel.

Emma Fish (10)
Our Lady of Hartley RC Primary School

The Alphabet

A is for Alfie who eats apples.
B is for Ben who bounces balls.
C is for Chloe who cares for cats.
D is for David who likes to play darts.
E is for Ella who cleans the cellar.
F is for Fran who likes to go frantic.
G is for Gemma who likes gems.
H is for Hannah who likes ham.
I is for Iona who likes ice.
J is for Joanna who likes jam.
K is for Katie who likes to kick.
L is for Linda who likes a lolly.
M is for Miranda who likes her mum.
N is for Neil who likes to nick.
O is for Oliver who likes to cook.
P is for Peter who picks at his food.
Q is for the Queen who curtsies.
R is for Richard who is rich.
S is for Slither who's my pet snake.
T is for Tim who likes to play tennis.
U is for umbrella that lives in a cellar.
V is for Violet who is violent.
W is for window-man who cleans the windows.
X is for X-ray to see your bones.
Y is for yo-yo that winds you down.
Z is for Zak who rides zebras.

Amy Rowe (9)
Our Lady of Hartley RC Primary School

I'm Going To Tell You A Tale

I'm going to tell you a tale
of a mixed up fairy tale
where horses and queens eat kings and mince
and the princess ends up kissing the prince

I'm going to tell you a yarn
where kings live in barns
where monsters are nice harmless fellows
and the Scottish end up playing the bellows

I'm going to tell you a fable
where everything has a label
where Jack and Jill fall up the hill
and a dragon ends up as a boy called Bill

I'm going to tell you a novel
where King Arthur grovels
where King Richard III gets even worse
and that's the end of my silly little verse.

Humphrey Heylen (9)
Our Lady of Hartley RC Primary School

Football Kennings

Goal-scorer
Dirty-tackler
Classic-header
Perfect-penalty
Shot-saver
Fantastic-defender
Wicked-defender
Fouling-players
Attacking-attackers
Right-backs.

Callum Sullivan (8)
Our Lady of Hartley RC Primary School

Homework

Home, home, I'm finally home
No, no it's the worst day of my life

Help, help, it's homework today
Help me God don't make me do it today

Home, home, you've always been the best
Do it for me, just don't make me do it today

You wouldn't, you wouldn't
You know it's chore day

Don't worry I have a plan
Just run away and don't come back today

I know I shouldn't, but I can't help it
I'll pick up the phone and find a friend

Oh no, the phone's packed up
It's already half six, I'll soon be going to bed

I've got to do something
I've got a plan I'll go to bed.

Jonathan Andrew Watts (9)
Our Lady of Hartley RC Primary School

Football

F antastic fullback
O fficials flagging for offside
O n a Saturday
T otti vs Terry, Terry the tackler
B allack vs Bent, Bellamy vs Beckham
A debayor scores for Arsenal
L ennon the loser
L junberg the best.

Rory McHugh (9)
Our Lady of Hartley RC Primary School

My Family

My mum is thin,
    but smaller than a pin!
My dad is tall
    and always has a fall!

My brother is clever,
    but is scared of a feather!
My sister is called Lily
    and is very silly!

My grandad sleeps a lot,
    but is always very hot!
My auntie is nice,
    but hates a spice!

My uncle is fat
    and wears a big hat!
My nanny is funny
    and has a white bunny!

My cousin is small
    and is as round as a ball!
Oh and me, well,
    I am just great!

Natalia Meeks (9)
Our Lady of Hartley RC Primary School

Fishing

F ishing is great fun
I need lots of tackle
S ome fish get foul hooked
H aving carp to eat
I nside some fishes' mouths, there isn't always teeth
N ymphs and flies will catch the trout
G etting a decent fish is great fun.

Daniel Blatchford (8)
Our Lady of Hartley RC Primary School

Spider, Spider

Spider, spider on the wall,
I could see you,
But now there's two.
I don't know which one's who,
Fine, then I'll play your game,
I'll ask your name,
Then I'll ask mine again.
Now I know because
The other one has a long nose.
When I touch you,
You go boo,
Then when I touch the other one,
You go who.
The word you tried to say
Is boo-hoo.
I am sorry
That I hurt you,
But now I now there's two,
I want to see you.

Juan Pocholo Cabling (7)
Our Lady of Hartley RC Primary School

Playground

P retty flowers on the grass
L ovely children playing
A lovely quiet area
Y ellow leaves in autumn
G irls skipping
R ustling leaves
O n the playground
U nder the trees there is grass
N o running in the quiet area
D on't you love the playground?

Joseph Dowsett (7)
Our Lady of Hartley RC Primary School

My Favourite Place

My favourite place is Fairyland.
I can see lots of yummy treats
And fairies and elves playing with Shonon and I.
I can see the blue sky
And the candyfloss clouds.
I can hear the bells ringing in the cake and sweet shops.
Gingerbread men talking to each other.
I can feel the fresh air
And the super yummy floor.
I can also see the party fairies,
Their names are Polly, Cherry, Jasmine, Honey, Grace,
                                    Melodie and Phoebe.
I can taste the yummy cakes and sweets.

Sukirti Lohani (8)
Our Lady of Hartley RC Primary School

Playground

P eaceful playground
L eaves falling down
A nimals hibernating
Y ellow, brown and gold leaves
G reen grass
R ed sky in the morning, shepherd's warning
O h fluffy clouds
U nder warm clothes
N obody around
D on't be found.

Jack Wigmore (8)
Our Lady of Hartley RC Primary School

A Bad Day

My sister's gone mad,
My brother won't get up,
My dad's lost his wallet
And my mum won't co-operate!

I'm trying to get to school,
My dog's sniffing his toy,
My hamster won't stop biting the cage
And the baby's giving me a headache!

I'm finally at school,
My teacher keeps telling me off,
My friends are leaving me out
And my lunch is all mouldy!

People are making my work book wet,
Somebody's stolen my pen,
No one will play with me
And people are hitting me!

The school just phoned my mum
And told her to come and collect me,
But she won't comply,
Nor will my dad!

Finally it's home time,
My mum's coming to get me,
My brother's in the car crying
And my dog's barking his head off.

What a *bad* day!

Natalya Silva (9)
Our Lady of Hartley RC Primary School

My House

My house is my favourite place,
I go to it every day.
I sleep in it,
I get dressed in it,
I even stay there every day.

I smell my yummy dinner cooked by my mum.
People come round our house.
I like school friends coming round.
I love my house,
I bet everyone does too.

I've got a cat.
I hear the TV going on.
I see the bedrooms for bedtimes.
You know I sleep in it don't you?
I love my house.
I really do,
Don't you?

Chloe Gardiner (7)
Our Lady of Hartley RC Primary School

My Best Place

My best place in the world is Lanzarote,
I can see the sea with the waves going gently over the sand,
I can see the children kicking up sand,
I can hear the birds tweeting in the trees,
I can hear the people splashing in the water,
But do you know what I can feel?
I feel the wind blowing in my hair
And the water splashing on me,
But I can also feel the heat burning my face,
I can taste chips,
I can smell the cold, chilly water,
But I can see you too.

Rian Sharkey (7)
Our Lady of Hartley RC Primary School

My Dream Place

My dream place is Disneyland.
When I go on the rides I can see people
Eating their lunch in a restaurant.
I see in the distance a train coming towards us.
I can see some children meeting the lovely, beautiful princess.

I can hear children shouting.
I can hear birds singing, 'A deer, a female deer.'
I smell cakes,
I smell fresh air,
I feel quite chilly,
I feel my hair blowing in the wind,
I touch the grass,
I touch my food.
That's the stuff I do at my best place in the world.

Emily James (7)
Our Lady of Hartley RC Primary School

My Dream Place

My favourite place is a make-believe place,
No people live there, but there is a unicorn,
The unicorn smells like fluffy white candyfloss.
When I go to bed I dream of it,
It seems like I've been there.
In my dreams there is a beautiful fairy,
She hears Christmas mint candy canes melting.
She never sees horrible, chocolate-brown, squelchy mud,
But she really wants to,
Especially the school that she goes to.
Nearly everything in her fairy school is chocolate colour
And she nearly ate some of it.
She loves Sweet Land.
That is the name of the place
And I love it too.

Shannon Penny (7)
Our Lady of Hartley RC Primary School

At Home

Flying birds,
Beeping a horn,
Leaves falling,
Smelling tea,
Playing in the garden,
Jumping up and down,
Fluffy clouds,
Wind blowing,
Cosy clothes,
Fluffy hats,
Warm, scary, cosy house,
Fire on,
A warm bed,
My daddy kisses me, bedtime.

Charlotte Heylen (7)
Our Lady of Hartley RC Primary School

My Favourite Place

My favourite place is Candy Land.
When I stand there I can see
Fairies playing games
And Ginger the fairy shopping.
There's a shop full of sweets
And it's made of sweets.
When I stand there I can hear
The candy ice cream truck,
Come round singing a soft song
And I can hear sweet birds singing in a sweet tree.
When I stand there I can touch
The soft ice cream tree
And the giant cherry cake.
When I stand there I can taste
The sweet fresh air
And the smoke of the candy factory.

Bryony Knight (7)
Our Lady of Hartley RC Primary School

Outside

Birds tweeting,
Aeroplanes flying,
Leaves scrunching,
Bumpy playgrounds,
Swaying trees,
Playpens,
Cars whizzing,
Squidgy mud,
Floating leaves,
Daisies floating,
Footsteps,
Wind dancing,
Fresh air,
Climbing frames,
Children run.

Fay Rendall (7)
Our Lady of Hartley RC Primary School

Key Blade

K ey Blade is so powerful
I diots running in and out of the world
N arla is a lion
G oofy is a dog
D onald is a duck
O ctopus making music
M ickey is the king

H eartless keep on dying
E ric is saved in a storm
A laddin is a street rat
R oxas was not meant to exist
T ron is a computer genius
S ora is the Key Blade master.

Dom Fernley (8)
Our Lady of Hartley RC Primary School

Jump In!

Leaves
Crunchy leaves
Crunchy, scrunchy leaves
Crunchy, scrunchy, crispy leaves
Crunchy, scrunchy, crispy, whirling leaves
Crunchy, scrunchy, crispy, whirling, golden leaves
Crunchy, scrunchy, crispy, whirling, golden, carmine leaves.

Lawura Sanda-Bah
Our Lady of Hartley RC Primary School

Chelsea

C aptain being cheered
H eart thumping
E xcited for us to win, a goal for Chelsea
L ampard scores for Chelsea!
S lide-tackling the other team
E verybody singing
A win for Chelsea.

Cameron Johl (8)
Our Lady of Hartley RC Primary School

Stars

Stars
Are the best,
Pretty little stars are glamorous
Silver and gold, shining in space,
What a lovely sight,
Glistening and gleaming,
Sparkling in space,
Everyone loves stars!
They are like
The moon's
Children.

Amber Matthews (8)
Our Lady of Hartley RC Primary School

Life Under The Sea

Under the sea
I'll tell you . . . crystal clean water,
Magic and secret caves,
There are dolphins to take creatures for sea,
Do you know what's going on?
Maybe it's a place full of mermaids and rides,
Rainbowfish jumping to make rainbows,
Under the sea, water palaces are made of crystal,
Pearls are precious jewels in secret caves,
Starfish are so shiny, gleaming, glistening,
Shells are one of the lovely things there,
Seaweed is like new socks,
Octopuses are so old,
Jellyfish are waiting to sting,
Whales and penguins are so lovely,
Sea horses, buried treasure, sunken ship,
Rays, clownfish and schools of them too,
Anemones are the best for me,

That's what's under the sea,
Go find out yourself . . . go, I dare you!

Fionnuala Joseph (8)
Our Lady of Hartley RC Primary School

Leaves

Leaves red
Yellow, orange
Gold and green

Leaves are a
Blanket of colour
A coat for a tree

Leaves crunchy
Ripped, crispy
Torn and beautiful

Leaves are joy.

Jack Watson (8)
Our Lady of Hartley RC Primary School

The Deep Sea

The deep blue sea goes
Down and down with lots of different colours
The blue, foamy waves hit the bay with a whisper
But in a storm they roar

Down at the bottom of the deep
The coral sways and swerves
And in that coral you can find clownfish in their homes
Then the graceful seal comes and shows a spectacular display

The deep blue sea is full of surprises
Pearls in oysters, fish to eat
And secrets waiting to be discovered
I wonder if you can uncover a secret of the deep?

Ciara Doyle (8)
Our Lady of Hartley RC Primary School

The Car

There was once a car, an evil car,
It caused terror far and wide,
It was big and black,
With blacked-out windows,
Whoever's driving can't be stopped,
It's a danger to be sure,
No one's driving, look at it go,
Throwing people to and fro.
It kills one person,
Moves on to another,
It's going too fast
Off a cliff,
That's a big fireball,
It's a screaming face.
There was once a car, an evil car,
It caused terror far and wide.

Oscar Betts (9)
Rolvenden Primary School

You Might Get A Fright

In the moonlight at night
You might get a fright in the night
A bird or bat on a mat
It shows its teeth and they're flat
Bony skeleton running mad at night
Help! Help!
Shout to all the people in town
Ghosts float through the doors at night

Witches screeching
Vampires sucking blood
Werewolves barking at the light
You might get a fright in the night!
Pumpkins come alive firing fireballs at night
Look for meat, it's the wizards
Church bells ringing wakes the gargoyle
'Roar,' goes the dragon at night
Dinosaurs coming back to life
Eating meat at night
That's why you might get a fright.

Robert Ward (9)
Rolvenden Primary School

My Monster

He's green, hairy and very scary,
He has razor sharp teeth,
He bellowed his bellow as loud as he could,
He laughed and laughed, the creep,
His deep red blood could cause a flood,
Yes deep red blood,
His green wrinkly skin,
He fell in a bin of toxic waste,
He's got four arms, four legs, six eyes.
When he knocks, you're bound to fall on the floor, *argh!*

Millie Goad (9)
Rolvenden Primary School

I've Spilt My Food

I've
  spilt
    my
      food
        all
          up
            my
              vest.
               It
            will
          need
        a
      wash
    a
    splash
   and
  a
splosh.
    I've
      made
      a
        mess
       a
        mess.

Rebecca Talbot (9)
Rolvenden Primary School

Summer

Puff! Puff!
Off she goes,
Round the bushes, trees, houses, ditches,
The sun is shining everywhere,
There's a man digging up crops over there.
There goes summer everywhere.

Rosie Masters (9)
Rolvenden Primary School

Dolphins Are Good Pets

Dolphins
flip, dive
and swim.
They live
in the sea.
You can
adopt them
and swim
with them
in Paris.
So go to Paris,
and swim
in the dolphin pool.
Swim away,
train them,
watch them feed,
throw them fish
and balls.

Kelly Ann Hedges (9)
Rolvenden Primary School

A Demon's Dinner

Cockroaches are good, they are fun,
They are excellent for my tum.
I like to eat legs,
As long as they're not pegs.
An eye is tasty, but they make me run up the wall,
It makes my friends think I'm a fool.
Toenails are nice
And they last briefly with rice.
Guns make me fat,
But I'm literally flat.

Luke Piggott (10)
Rolvenden Primary School

Scissors - From All Angles

From above:
A pair of eyes and a huge mouth,
Like a giant monster.

From the side:
A smooth silver river,
As tall as a giraffe.

From the front:
The nose of a dolphin,
Peaking up from out of the water.

Rhianna Hodgkins (9)
Rolvenden Primary School

A Goat Is Loose

A goat is loose,
A goat is loose,
Through the gate and onto the road,
What a silly goat he is,
Because he is heading towards troll bridge
And now he is gone.
The troll is now coming for you.

Jacky Hunt (10)
Rolvenden Primary School

A Fire-Breathing Dragon

A fire-breathing dragon roaring in fear,
Really angry, drinking beer,
Eating a child mixed up with trifle,
Chewing along with a munch and munch
And the person is dead!

Kajun Stannard (8)
Rolvenden Primary School

Beaches

The sandy, sometimes gritty ground,
The crabs in shells all safe and sound,
Umbrellas green, blue and red,
A sign saying seagulls not to be fed,
People on picnics eating different fruits,
No need now for Wellington boots,
Running races to the ice cream van,
Having races as fast as they can,
Collecting shells in plastic bags,
Building sandcastles with coloured flags,
People waving buckets and spades,
Unrolling huge new sunshades,
Running in the deep, deep sand,
Listening to the jolly band.

But the year does grow on
And soon the summer fun is gone,
People pack their things away
And no one comes to spend the day.

Wrap up warm and walk the dog,
No one else is there in the fog,
Wear your scarf, gloves and hat,
All gone are the places where people sat,
In winter dogs are off their lead,
Sniffing at bits of old seaweed,
The nights are darker and days are cold
And the big lighthouse is getting old.

Of both these beaches I prefer,
The golden beach in the summer.

Joanna Harvey (10)
Shernold School

Babysitting!

When you go to babysit,
The child may scream and shout,
Don't spoil them with cakes and sweets,
Because they may get mad and run about.

If they are a baby then rock them to sleep,
If they awaken they may be like a car,
Crashing through the traffic,
Beep, beep, beep!

Here comes back the mummy,
The child is fast asleep,
But the great thing about this is,
The pocket money!

Katie Swift (9)
Shernold School

Mouse

There was a furry brown mouse that was tame
Who was the prime minster of Spain
He was very strong
But he never said it was wrong
As he liked being tough
But if someone annoyed him, he got the huff
And everyone liked him a lot
Even Mr Cot who always lost the plot

He was always twitching
But never itching
As he kept himself clean
And ate his greens
So he always kept himself healthy
And he was very wealthy.

Laura Morton (8)
Shernold School

The Kite

I run into the house
Get my coat
Grab the kite from the shed
It flies really high
High in the sky
It's blue, white and red

It takes off from the ground
Into the sky
Swishing and swashing
Flying right by
Turning around
Flying up high
My fast kite doing tricks in the sky

It gets out of control
It's going to crash
It spins round and round
Then hits the ground
I need to go in to have my tea
Who's going to pack away my kite for me?

Thomas Collins (8)
Shernold School

My Dog

I have a dog called Jack,
He has a hairy back,
He has a hairy front as well,
It's sometimes difficult to tell,
Which way round his head has gone,
Or even if he has got one!

George Quinn (8)
Shernold School

My Journey Through Space

When I look upon the stars
I can see the moon and Mars.
Look at all the blue and black,
In a few years I'll be back.

A galaxy so far away,
I can see the Milky Way.
Jupiter and Saturn await
As I speed through the star gate.

My spaceship is so silver and red,
I'll never know when it's time for bed.
It's always dark up here in space,
I feel the G-force on my face.

And now it's the end
Of my wonderful roam,
I say goodbye to you all
As I come back home.

Daniel Sharp (10)
Shernold School

My Favourite Thing

My favourite thing in the world . . .
On top he is curled.
I have one of these,
But yet I never hear him sneeze.
On top he has a shell,
He never smells!
His name is Toby,
He moves very slowly.

Have you guessed yet . . . ?
Well . . . it's a tortoise,
Toby is my pet tortoise.

Connor Rumball (9)
Shernold School

I Love To Dance

I love to dance
To Latin and hip-hop
I love to dance
And I never want to stop
I love to dance

I love to dance
All day long
I love to dance
When it's a loud song
I love to dance

I love to dance
When the sky is blue
I love to dance
In time with you.

I love to dance.

Aaliyah Buxy (7)
Shernold School

Hedgehogs

Hedgehogs live in a hollow tree
Every night they go out to see
Dogs might give them such a fright
Go and see them roll up tight
Eat as slug
Have a bug
On their backs lots of spines
Great and sharp
So don't touch its back
Or it will prickle.

Anujan Ravishankar (7)
Shernold School

Sunny Florida

F lorida is a sunny city in the USA
L ots of tourists come every day
O ranges are ripe and ready to be picked off the trees
R ides are fun but also scary
I n the park you can watch the parades
D rinking because it's hot, sitting in the shade
A merica is the best place to be!

Lilyan Mashallah (8)
Shernold School

Bunnies

Bunnies are a kind of animal,
Nice and furry, nice to cuddle,
A kind of animal that likes to run and jump about,
An animal that likes to eat any kind of vegetable.
They have big ears that are sometimes floppy,
My favourite kind of bunny is a lop-eared.
Sometimes they bite,
They don't like being picked up.

Constance Fury (7)
Shernold School

Monkey Rhyme

Monkeys swinging in a tree,
They all call for a cup of tea,
They all fall in a pot!
One blue, one red and one white
And that is the end of the monkey rhyme!

Jemima Burn (7)
Shernold School

My Doll's House

I've got a pretty doll's house,
It's white and pink and red,
It sits up in my bedroom,
Right next to my bed.

Lots of little people
Live in the pretty house,
There's Mummy and there's Daddy,
Seven children and a mouse.

All the children have a pet
That lives beneath the table,
They even have a pony
Who lives out in the stable.

I wish that I were little,
So I could live there too,
It's such a happy place to be
Because there's lots of things to do.

Amelia Lucy Gregory (7)
Shernold School

My Fairy Friends

Can you see the fairies dancing on my bed?
Little wings and pretty skirts with flowers on their heads,
They creep up close beside me and cuddle up all night,
Dreaming of things that glitter, while the moon is shining bright.
When Mummy comes to say, 'Goodnight,' the fairies hide away,
But when it's just me and them I know they will come to play.
Little girls see fairies as clearly as can be,
Little friends to share in all my fantasies.

Bethany Joanne Tompsett (7)
Shernold School

Two Spiders

Two spiders dangling down my ceiling,
One chubby fat,
One skinny slim.

The two met up ready to fight,
One gave a karate kick,
One gave a heavy punch with all its might.

The two were exhausted, they had a break,
One crawled nervously back home,
One limped home with an ache.

After the break they met face to face,
One gave a friendly shake,
One returned a gentleman's bow,
The two made up and became mates!

Keri Mo (7)
Shernold School

Witches

Witches are black and grey,
They love to sleep all day,
They adore black cats,
They have tall pointy hats!

They boil little girls
And turn them into dark circles,
Witches are black and grey,
They love to sleep all day!

At night they zoom into the sky
And then they say bye!

Rebecca-Kate Lawley Watts (9)
Shernold School

Cats

Sleepy cats,
lie on mats,
they like to snooze
in the morning sun.

When they awake
they like to stretch,
then they choose
to chase around,
causing havoc
on the ground.

They scurry and
they scamper,
they hide, then they
pounce.

Then they've got you
and there we go,
they've got you.

All snuggled in your arms
there they rest and close their eyes
and go back to their dreams.

Robert Lawrence (10)
Shernold School

My Big Head

My name is Fred and I've got a big head
I like to eat toasted bread,
I live in a shed and I sleep in a bed,
And I hit my head on a lump of lead
'So that is why I have got a big head,' said Fred!

Vinnie Iandolo (7)
Shernold School

Homework On Fridays

Why do we have homework?
Really, what's the point?
Maths and English,
Sometimes science too!

Maths drives me mad!
All the sums and adding up,
Division's worst!
Why do we have to do it?

English isn't so bad,
But it's bad all the same,
Prefixes and suffixes,
Handwriting's worst.

Science is best of all,
There's only one downside to it,
Learning about blood,
It all just adds to Friday.

Why do we have homework?
Well at least mine is finished!
Just maths and English,
Aren't you bored with it?

Jasmine Ede (9)
Shernold School

Harvest

H arvest is when the leaves start to fall,
A time when farmers pick all the fruit and vegetables,
R ed, juicy apples fall so people can pick them,
V ery poor people get the money that we spend.
E very harvest we think of God and everyone,
S ome animals start to get ready for the winter,
T he store is ready for winter and we should also remember
                                    about the poor.

Zenon Ede (7)
Shernold School

My Puppy Keano

I bought a puppy called Keano,
I was going to call him Deano.
I bought him home, he cried alone,
Poor old little Keano.

When I woke up, I went downstairs
And there was my little Keano.

I saw some poo and some wee
And cleaned it up on my knees.

I had to go to school,
Keano stood like a stool
When I went out the door.

I came home that day
And my dog was happy today.

I bought a puppy called Keano.

Garren Beaulieu (10)
Shernold School

Grace

I've got a cousin called Grace,
She has short brown hair with a pretty round face.

She has a mum, dad and a baby brother
And Grace and I share the same grandmother.

Grace is eight soon to be nine,
She will never catch up with me and that's fine.

We sometimes play and sometimes fight,
But most of the time we are friends and that's alright.

Danielle Wheat (10)
Shernold School

My Cats

My cats are black,
My cats are white,
My cats are black and white,
Some cats are multicoloured,
But some are just plain white.

Some cats are fat,
Some cats are thin,
Some cats are long,
Some cats are short,
But mine are just right.

My cats' paws are white,
Some cats' paws are black,
Some cats' paws are multicoloured,
But mine are just white.

Their faces are black,
Their faces are white,
Their faces are black and white
And my cats are just right.

I did have three but
I now only have two,
As one sadly died,
But now it's just two.

Abbie Prentice (10)
Shernold School

Clocks

It has a face,
No eyes or mouth,
Hands go round,
It makes no sound,
Only when it strikes the hour.

George Durrant (9)
Shernold School

My Dog Rusty

My dog is mad
And very bad,
He always wants to play,
He can jump really high
And can reach the sky,
He gets higher every day.

He tries to be good,
When he wants some food,
He sits and begs,
It never lasts long,
When the food is gone,
He runs around on four legs.

Even though he is trouble,
We love to cuddle.
He comes when I call his name,
He is my friend,
Right to the end,
Even though he is a pain!
'Rusty, sit!'

Chloe Rogers (8)
Shernold School

The Roller Coaster

The roller coaster twisting and turning
Up and down
Left and right
Nearly touching the ground
Quick and slow
Upside down
Straight and bumpy
Scream and shout.

Anna Holness (7)
Shernold School

Beep Goes The Car

Beep goes the car,
Puff goes the train,
Honk goes the clown's nose, red as a cherry.

Crash goes the plates,
Flap goes the wings,
Squelch goes the cake mixture falling to the floor.

Neigh goes the horse,
Baa goes the sheep,
Buzz goes the bee flying to and fro.

Whistle goes the wind,
Tweet goes the bird,
Shout goes the crowd when we score a goal.

These are the sounds of the world today
And I love them so,
I wonder what we'll hear tomorrow.

Sophie Burn (10)
Shernold School

My Best Friend Ciara

She is always there for me
She is my best friend
She loves football
She is my best friend
She has two baby sisters
She is my best friend
She has brown hair
She is my best friend
That's why she is my best friend.

Ellena Jepheart (8)
Shernold School

Jack And Jill Went To The Mall

Jack and Jill went over the wall,
To fetch some clothes from the shopping mall,
Jack went into a lift instead of a shop,
Jill ran over to the stairs and looked over the top.
It was very high, you could say she was hitting the sky.
She leaned even further, let me put it like this,
She felt the full force of the drop.
When Jack exited the lift he got caught in the door,
So they both went splat on the ground floor

Moral

Dear children don't look over the top of the stairs,
Also be first out of the lift, don't hang around in there!

Chloe Funnell (10)
Shernold School

The Clear Blue Sky

The sky is as blue and as clear as the sea,
But not like a scared mouse up a tree.

The clouds are not blue but they're part of the sky,
The cat is as sly as the blink of an eye.

The part of the sky that is never blue,
We don't know do you?

Although the sky is not always blue,
You're not going to go *woo woo.*

In the morning the sky makes me feel happy,
The clouds, the birds.

At night the sky is not as happy because
You don't see the cheerfulness.

Jack Bates (10)
Shernold School

Scary Hallowe'en Is On Its Way

Guess what?
I saw ghosts, demons, witches, wizards and all sorts
I saw blood dripping from a vampire's teeth
Witches flying on their broomsticks
Wizards making potions
Demons playing their parts
Pumpkins being lit
Children starting to get scared
And trick or treating never to forget
Pots being broken, eggs thrown at doors
Are you starting to believe?
Do you feel scared? Are you terrified?
If I were you I would want to hide

Don't worry, calm down
Please don't frown
It's just a Hallowe'en party.

Jasmin Major (8)
Shernold School

My Mum

My mum is pretty and has brown eyes
She is nice
My mum is cheerful and lots of fun
She is great
My mum is a wonderful cook
She is brill
My mum plays tennis and swims
She is fit
My mum likes flowers indoors
She is very, very nice!

Isabelle Knight (7)
Shernold School

My Cat

I have a cat that is kind,
He has a very good mind.

I have a cat that is cool,
He plays rough and tumble with a ball.

I have a cat that is loud,
He struts around very proud.

I have a cat that is small,
He can stretch out very tall.

I have a cat called Sam
And he eats all the ham.

But when he gets in trouble he goes *miaow!*

Dominic Le Lion (10)
Shernold School

Seasons

Seasons come and seasons go,
But I can't wait until it snows.
Snowball fights everywhere
And snow gets stuck in my hair.

Jack Frost sitting on my lawn,
It's harvest time, don't forget your corn!

Blossom floating in the sky,
The smell of spring and kites flying high.

I love summer, ice cream and treats for me,
Running and jumping in my pool,
Lots of laughing, that sounds cool!

Charlotte Wilson (8)
Shernold School

University!

My sister is going to university,
All my friends say, 'It's a monster going to eat her.'
But she still wants to go.
Mum said it cost a lot of money.
She has packed up to leave,
But I don't want her to.
She said she will be back soon,
She said she has to work hard.
Gone for winter,
Gone from me,
All things we used to do,
Play,
Talk,
Ride my bike.
She has gone off to study now,
I miss her so much.
Three more years,
Just three,
Only three.

Matilda Duffy (10)
Shernold School

My Lamborghini

I want a Murciélago because when I drive to school
I feel like an escargot!

I want to go fast, I want to whizz past cars
On the way to school.

It bores, it snores me, driving this slow
I wish I could go, go, go.

Oh I so want my Murciélago
But you know what I'd settle for a Gallardo.

Jack Wilson (8)
Shernold School

Fitz And Fred

Fitz and Fred are my dogs,
They do enjoy chewing on logs,
They run around patrolling the grounds,
But when they sleep all is sound.

Fred is a beagle,
With the eyes of an eagle,
Fitz, a Labrador,
Who just likes to snore.

When dinnertime awaits,
You'll find they are never late,
When they go to bed,
They rest their little heads.

When I arrive home from school,
The dog begins to drool,
They pick things off the ground,
Saying look what I have found.

I love my dogs completely,
Their names are Fitz and Fred,
I fold their blankets neatly,
When it's time to go to bed.

Gemma Levy (10)
Shernold School

Me And My Mum

When Daddy takes my brother to football
Me and Mummy go out to shop
Sometimes we go to the cinema
Sometimes we go to the park
I like it when they go to football
I can have Mummy all to myself
We can snuggle up on the sofa
And not listen to them shout.

Jade Richards (7)
Shernold School

Horses

Horses are my favourite animals,
Boys don't like horses,
But I really do,
You should like them too.

My favourite horse is black,
She has a white spot upon her back,
She has a big, white, bushy tail
And her favourite food is snails.

The horse sleeps in a stable,
It has no chairs or tables,
Just a room full of hay,
That's where the horse loves to lay,
All day!

Isabel Peterson (7)
Shernold School

The Glamorous Girls

Gemma is totally funny
and loaded with money.

Sophie is seriously mad
and sometimes really bad.

Chloe our tomboy of the group
a great cook with a wonderful soup!

Abbie your CKD girl
will make your hair curl.

Alice just plain old me
Writing this poem with a cup of tea.

Alice Jepheart (10)
Shernold School

My Special Friend

I have a special friend
He has four legs and a tail
His nose is wet and black
And his coat is soft and pale.

I take him for long walks
I cuddle him a lot
I feed him lots of snacks
And fill up his water pot.

He has two huge eyes
They are brown and very kind
And if I'm a bit sad
He can always read my mind.

He likes to lick my hand
And loves going for a walk
I like to tickle him
And he loves it when we talk.

He whines a lot at night
When he wants to come upstairs
But he can't get up
Cos we block the way with chairs.

Whenever I come back
He runs to get a toy
It's a present for me
From my lovely boy!

His name is Nelson
He is eleven years old
He is my very special friend
And he will never be sold.

Natalie Ashby (8)
Shernold School

Hallowe'en Warning!

Zombies, ghosts and monsters
Come out to play tonight
They creep around in the dark
Hoping to give you a fright!

If they come and find you
You had better just run away
Because you can bet your life
You won't like the games they play!

It's safer to stay at home
With all the lights on full
Don't go trick or treating
Or you might not come back at all!

Alex Elliott (9)
Shernold School

A Child

When someone says child,
A chirpy voice comes to my mind.
When someone says child,
Soul and life comes to my mind.

A child's way is full of light,
A child's face is full of glory,
A child's heart is full of love,
Do not break that way of love.

A child is the cheer of your home,
A child is the chirpiness of your home.
A child wants love,
A child is the way of happiness.

Ahsen Ustaóglu (10)
Shernold School

Paint

'Share the bright coloured paints,
You should have your own brushes,'
Our teacher said as she left,
Then everyone rushes

To get the best set.
While the teacher's away,
Carl I bet,
Will ruin my day.

'Out of my way!'
The bully gave a scream,
As he gave me a shove,
He's so horrid and mean.

Drip, drip, splodge,
Oh no what a mess!
Bright red paint
Down my new school dress.

Here comes Carl
Dripping paint everywhere,
It's all over my work
And the teacher is there.

The teacher said, 'Time's up,
Put your work on my table.'
She thought that mine was very good,
I got first prize, joint with Mabel.

I hope that Carl will help me
Next time we have to paint,
I've changed my mind about him now,
He's really quite a saint.

Ruth Arnett (9)
Shernold School

My Twin Sisters

Naughty girls come in pairs,
Twins is their name.
They come in different sizes,
But they both just look the same.

They can sit and they can stand,
They are always crawling about.
They like to play with toys,
They like to scream and shout.

Twins like to climb,
On our baby door,
But they cry so much
When they fall on the floor.

Nihal is one,
Neval's the other
And in the night,
They cause Mum a bother.

Neval is younger,
So Nihal is older
And when they were born,
Neval was bolder.

Ali Sever (9)
Shernold School

The Dragon

I know a dragon that's big and green,
Every time he roars we all scream.
He's big and tall and very strong,
Don't let him catch you doing anything wrong.
When he breathes, out comes fire, hot enough to melt a tyre.
This enormous dragon has an enormous tail,
Our favourite dragon comes from Wales.

Jacob Bischoff (7)
Shernold School

Family Life

Mummies

Mummies are good,
Mummies are kind,
Mummies' jobs are never done,
That's why we have so much fun.

Daddies

Daddies work just as hard,
Working in a big toy yard,
Some daddies work on a boat,
Or some wear a great big coat.

Children

Children just go to school
And play with a gigantic ball,
Whoever you are don't be sad,
Just be jolly and always glad.

Charlotte Rugg-Gunn (8)
Shernold School

The Mighty Jungle

Going through the jungle trees here and there,
I can see a monkey and then I see a bear.
I can see a lion sleeping on a log,
Then I see a lily pad and on jumps a frog.
I can see a squirrel running up a tree,
Then I see a wild cat going for a wee!
I can see a crocodile splashing in a lake,
Then I see a person whose back really aches.
After a day's walk I climb into my bed
And say to myself, 'All the animals have fed.'

James Sharp (9)
Shernold School

My Baby Cousin

My baby cousin is called Douglas Myers,
He is the cutest baby in the world!
He sometimes cries,
He is the cutest baby in the world!
He's got dark brown hair and big blue eyes,
He is the cutest baby in the world!
He drinks milk from a bottle,
He is the cutest baby in the world!
He sucks a dummy,
He is the cutest baby in the world!
He holds onto my finger when I cuddle him,
The only bad things about him are he has smelly nappies
And he cries and wakes up in the night!
But I still love him and kiss him to bits!

Maisy Cane (8)
Shernold School

What A Feeling

There is a feeling that's really cool,
When my left foot strikes the ball.

When it thunders towards the goal,
Swerving, curling out of control.

For the girls it might be a bore,
But for me the best feeling is to score.

A rasping, pounding, volleyed shot,
Makes me feel like I'm on top.

When I score everyone cheers
And the dads drink beers.

Ellis Iandolo (9)
Shernold School

Goodnight Little Fairy

If you ever see a fairy
Then this is what you'll see,
A tiny little body and a face full of glee.
Held in her hand is a little tiny wand
And she'll sit and she'll smile
Waiting by the pond.

She twinkles in the night
And glimmers like a star,
She waits like an angel
In the moonlight afar.

When you come she'll smile
And she'll say, 'I've waited a while!'
Quickly she sprinkles some dust into the night,
Then she shouts, 'Goodbye!'
And flies into the light.

Amelia C Peterson (9)
Shernold School

Fairies

We sing a song to the world below,
We sing a song to the rivers that flow.
We are the fairies in the sky,
Flying free and flying high.
The sky is filled with bright shining blue,
We grant wishes just for you.
If you make a wish today,
We will fly down and make it OK.
Oh! What's that noise?
Children shouting, 'Hooray.'

Elizabeth Elliott (7)
Shernold School

The Unicorn's Horn

The unicorn's horn
Shines in the moonlight
From the day he was born
Twinkling like stars at night.

The unicorn's horn
Is a magical sight
Like a twisting barley corn
Shining, shining ever so bright.

The unicorn's horn
Making mysterious shadows
Disappearing at dawn
Where does he go?
Back to our dreams, before a new day begins.

Chelsea Lauren Davison (9)
Shernold School

I Wish I Had A Brother

I wish I had a brother
To play with me all day long
Instead of my two sisters
Who drive me round the bend
We'd play football in the garden
Or build an army camp
Play with my two castles
With all my army men
I wish I had a brother
To wrestle with and fight
But I'd miss my two sisters
Because they've been here quite a while.

Harry Grindle (8)
Shernold School

My Dog Harry

I have a dog
His name is Harry
He is short and spotty
And very dotty

He loves to go on walks
And will do anything for a bone
He sleeps all day
He lies on his back
Hoping to get a scratch

He wags his tail
When he's happy
Harry is very clever
And I love him lots
This is my dog Harry!

Emily Watts (9)
Shernold School

The Robot Mum

Wouldn't it be great to have a robot mum
Who could do all your homework
And would never raise her voice when you have a messy room?
She would buy the latest designer clothes from Gap.
Robot Mum would take you to Burger King
And would never mind about your diet.

When I feel sad and glum, she gives me a hug,
But it feels all metallic and makes me feel worse.

I think I'll stick to my 'real' mum!

Miriam Aziz (9)
Shernold School

The Three Little Puppies

My three little puppies play in the house,
All day and night chasing a mouse.

My three little puppies watch telly,
As my mum puts on a welly.

My three little puppies look at the clock,
As it goes *tick-tock, tick-tock.*

My three little puppies stare at the ball,
They feel like they're going to fall.

My three little puppies sit and wait,
For food on their plate.

My three little puppies see a ring,
So they start to sing.

My three little puppies sit on a chair
And then go to the school fair.

My three little puppies have a talk
When they go for a walk.

Don't make a peep
Because my three little puppies have gone to sleep.

Sam Farmer (9)
Shernold School

My Mum

My mum is very kind,
She lets me ride my horse,
She cares for me and my brothers,
That's why I love her of course.

My mum is 39
And has a horrid brother,
Her brunette hair is lovely,
The same as her mother.

She looks after my sister,
Feeds her, you know,
Looks after my brothers too
And when Mum says, 'I've bought myself a horse,'
All they say is, 'So!'

My mum has lovely green eyes,
They look like the grass,
She says we never lie,
She has got a lovely past.

So that was a poem about my *mum*
She is as lovely as can be
It was written by her favourite child
Who can that be? *Me!*

Charlotte Beedell (9)
Shernold School

The Chicken Life

Being a chicken is great fun,
Although on occasions we act a little dumb!

Rooting around for worms all day,
Ruining the borders along the way.

Time comes to lay a big egg,
A tasty treat for my owner, Meg.

At teatime us chickens just love to eat,
Mixed corn is our favourite as a treat.

Bedtime comes when we all roast,
Sleep does give us such a boost!

When the daytime dawns, we look so cute,
The cock crows so loud, I wish he was on mute!

Jordan Tompsett (10)
Shernold School

Friendship

I have a very special friend her name is Lydia,
But I call her Lyd for short,
She has freckles and so do I,
I have a few light ones.
We both have blonde hair, it's pretty in bunches.
I remember the time we used to fight,
But we made it up to each other in the end.
Guess how many years we've known each other?
Her nickname is Squid it's just for fun.
She knows she can trust me
And I know I can trust her.

Megan Smith (8)
Shernold School

Autumn

Chestnuts falling to the ground,
Leaves going crispy golden,
Squirrels gathering nuts and berries,
Birds leaving for the south.

Conkers cracking out of their cases,
The weather starts to chill off,
Frosts in the morning,
People wrapping up in layers, scarves, gloves and hats.

Elisabeth Holness (10)
Shernold School

The Months

January keeps me near the fire,
February makes me get all wet,
March, the leaves are firing,
April, sun begins to blaze,
May, the flowers begin to show,
June, the petals are as soft as silk,
July, the ice cream is as sweet as sugar,
August greets me with a brilliant tan,
September pushes the sunshine away
And greets the rain clouds with a horrible day,
October cold sneaks out of the fridge,
November, all we can hear is the fireworks thumping,
December, finally now we can rest,
For St Nicholas is on his way,
Better get to bed!

Shanice Friday (11)
The Holy Family Catholic Primary School

Months

January is like a white sheet
February is a wind that sneaks
March marches in
April is like peachy skin
May, the sun shows its face
June is a nice place
July is my birthday
August makes the hay
September, the sun starts to say goodbye
October starts to sigh
November, clouds cover up the sky
December, we're eating lots of pies.

Beth White (10)
The Holy Family Catholic Primary School

Animals By Numbers

One is the cat who stole the food.
Two is the mouse who's in the mood.

Three is the dog who likes to dance.
Four is the sheep who's going to France.

Five is the pig who's very fat.
Six is the horse who sits on a mat.

Seven it's the snake that gave his money.
Eight is the bee who took some honey.

Nine is the newt who needed a flute.
Ten is a kitten who is very cute.

Lauren Ramsden (10)
The Holy Family Catholic Primary School